W9-BAT-399

THE ENCYCLOPEDIA
OF SPICES AND HERBS

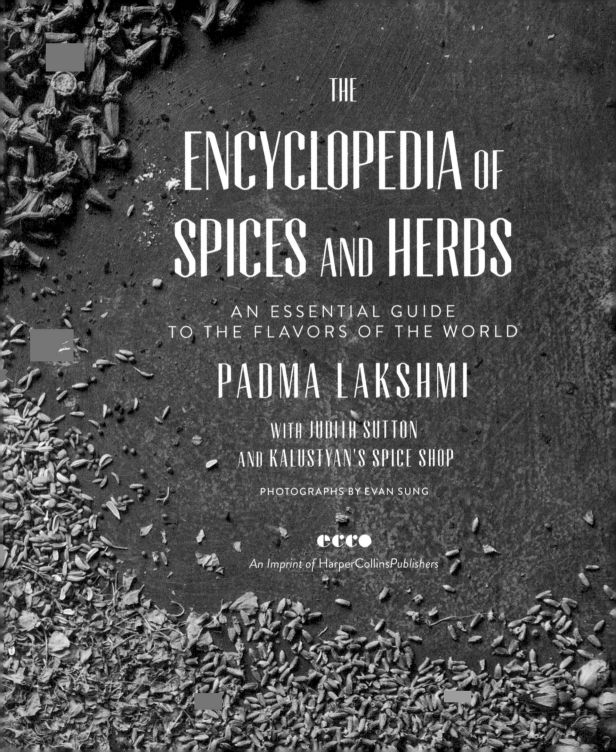

THE
ENCYCLOPEDIA OF
SPICES AND HERBS

AN ESSENTIAL GUIDE
TO THE FLAVORS OF THE WORLD

PADMA LAKSHMI

WITH JUDITH SUTTON
AND KALUSTYAN'S SPICE SHOP

PHOTOGRAPHS BY EVAN SUNG

ecco

An Imprint of HarperCollinsPublishers

HarperCollins books may be purchased for educational, business, or sales promotional use. For information please e-mail the Special Markets Department at SPsales@harpercollins.com.

FIRST EDITION

Designed by Suet Yee Chong

Library of Congress Cataloging-in-Publication Data has been applied for.

ISBN 978-0-06-237523-0

16 17 18 19 20   RRD   10 9 8 7 6 5 4 3 2 1

For Krishna,
my favorite cooking companion

CONTENTS

INTRODUCTION

Spices have always been part of my life. The black peppercorn, along with turmeric and ginger, comes from Kerala, the home of my ancestors, deep in the heart of South India. I can remember savoring its aroma in my grandmother's kitchen, the smell of the dry whole spices roasting in her iron wok as she made various curry powders from family recipes. The sound of tempering spices in hot oil, mustard seeds popping like rapid gunfire, sizzling fresh curry leaves, and the sharp, smoky haze of dried chiles—these sensations lured me into the kitchen, and I've remained there, among the canisters and jute sacks, ever since. Spices are something I feel almost born into; they awakened my nose and palate to the bounty of tastes and flavors awaiting me in the larger world.

But such bounty means that for every beloved flavor that can enhance a dish or re-create a memory, there are dozens more you've never seen or heard of. Once, twenty years ago, walking through the souk in Marrakesh for the first time, I was thrilled to find a stall with jars of bright green powders, twigs, garlands of nubby yellow roots, chunks of resins, and other treasures, which the shopkeeper, despite a lot of vigorous hand movements and grunts between us, could not describe to me in English. I packed as many of these as I could into my suitcase, ready to impress my loved ones and dinner guests, confident in my ability to make do with the knowledge and practice I already had. Until, back in my kitchen, I had no idea how any of it should be used—I felt lost. In India, I would have had one of the women in my family to guide me. They could sniff out the identity of anything I brought back to them. And in New York City, I would have gone back to the store I had spent years in as a child: Kalustyan's, on Lexington Avenue.

I began visiting Kalustyan's with my mother when I was four years old. She relied on the store whenever she ran low on the spices and herbs she expected to be fresh, aromatic, and authentic. Open since 1944, for many years Kalustyan's was the only purveyor in North America to sell Indian, Armenian, and Turkish spices and groceries. For a few generations of cooks, and many immigrants to the city, it was a singular culinary mecca, a place where you could always find anything; and if something wasn't there, the owners would make sure it was the next time you came in. They also plied delighted children with samples and sweets, like dates, Jordan almonds, and pieces of baklava, and still do today—when my own daughter walks through their door now, she runs loose, knowing she will have her fill of generous treats.

Kalustyan's initial success came because of two local Armenian churches and their parishioners, to whom the owner, K. Kalustyan, an Armenian himself, catered. But soon a whole community mushroomed around it, and the store became a vital enclave of immigrant life. I heard from my uncle Bharat, who emigrated to New York from India in the 1960s, about how precious Kalustyan's and its contents were to so many new New Yorkers during those first few years. In those days, he said, "It was a gift to have that store. We didn't have much else as a salve, to remind us of home, and take away our homesickness." In the mid-1970s, when the Murray Hill neighborhood around Kalustyan's began to change, Kalustyan's, then a small store, changed with it. A Bangladeshi man named Sayedul Alam, known as just Alam, opened a shop called Spice and Sweet Mahal on the corner, and down the street, Curry in a Hurry, a fast-casual restaurant outside of which you can still find a line of yellow cabs each day. In 1988, Alam and his cousin Aziz Osmani, also the current owners, took over Kalustyan's, along with 125 and 127 Lexington Avenue, which were added and now together house the large Kalustyan's store as it exists today. But I will always think of the address as its original: 123 Lexington Avenue.

When I moved to New York after college in the mid-1990s, the first place I went to fill my cupboards was Kalustyan's. And it was Kalustyan's I called long-distance from Milan when I needed help with my treasures from the Moroccan souk. I was spoiled in my young lifetime to have these two resources, my family and Kalustyan's, at my disposal. But what did others do?

To understand spices and their uses is to open a door to endless culinary possibility. Just as a good sorceress needs her book of spells, so, too, does a good cook need a compendium of seasonings and herbs to understand them. These potent parcels of flavor have been part of the very fabric of feeding ourselves for millennia, and yet most of us in the Western world still don't understand how to use many of them, where they came from, or how easy cooking with them can be. Consider the peppercorn, for example. This tiny fruit, a mighty bead of heat, has been a most potent catalyst of intrepid exploration and human history. It was these piquant spheres that made India and the rest of Southeast Asia so valuable to Europeans. The same is true for ginger, cassia and cinnamon, and many more spices. Whether a seed, flower, root, or bark, these elements of nature are responsible for shaping much of the world as we know it today. And in the culinary world, ingredients are being given new histories, incorporated into all kinds of dishes. All of a sudden, ginger and lemongrass have made their way into crème caramel and dessert sauces from Michelin-starred French chefs, American barbecue sauces contain chipotle peppers, and wasabi is being whipped into mashed potatoes at Thanksgiving.

I have always wanted a book like this, a reference guide that would tell me not only the provenance but also the uses of whatever spice or herb caught my attention. I wanted to harness all the things I had ever learned over years of combing through markets around the world and quizzing the different cooks and chefs I met along the way throughout my career in food. And I wanted to catalog and honor the encyclopedic breadth of Kalustyan's knowledge, gained over decades of serving their customers, hunting and gathering on behalf of curious New York cooks who come in, frazzled, with some recipe book or slip of paper in hand.

It's in this spirit that I am happy to introduce *The Encyclopedia of Spices and Herbs,* written with Judith Sutton and filled, of course, with sumptuous and helpful photographs of Kalustyan's products. We have tried our best to be clear, precise, and brief in the interest of our cooks, who may wander through these pages while planning a menu or preparing a meal in the kitchen. I'm confident you, too, will fall in love with the world of spices and herbs, and that the food you create will be changed for the better by a wealth of new additions to your pantry.

—Padma Lakshmi
New York, 2016

SPICES, HERBS, AND BLENDS
FROM A TO Z

ACHIOTE

See Annatto.

ADVIEH

OTHER SPELLINGS: adwiya

Advieh is a Persian spice blend that typically includes cumin, coriander, cinnamon, pepper, cardamom, cloves, nutmeg or mace, and ginger, as well as dried rosebuds or rose petals. Simpler versions may be made with only cumin, cardamom, cinnamon, and dried rose petals or buds; others may include all the spices mentioned above as well as turmeric; and still others use dried lemon peel. Advieh has a pungent aroma, a fine texture, and a warm brown color. It adds a rich flavor to couscous, pilafs, and other rice dishes. It also seasons Persian stews, lentil dishes, and soups; blends for stews may also include saffron. Advieh can be used as a dry rub for grilled or roasted meats. Stirred into yogurt or mixed with oil, it serves as a marinade for grilled meats and vegetables. Some blends are simply sprinkled over rice dishes as a garnish before serving rather than used to season them. In some Middle Eastern countries, a version of advieh is used to spice haroset, the fruit and nut paste that is part of the traditional Passover seder plate.

AJMUD/AJMOD

See Radhuni.

AJOWAN

BOTANICAL NAMES: *Trachyspermum ammi, Carum ajowan*
OTHER NAMES: ajwain, carom/carum, bishop's weed, lovage seeds (erroneously)
FORMS: whole seeds and ground

Ajowan is a member of the large Apiaceae family (formerly Umbelliferae) and a close relative of both parsley and caraway. Native to India and the eastern Mediterranean region, it is now also grown in Afghanistan, Egypt, Iran, and Pakistan, but India remains the major source. It is an annual herbaceous plant that resembles parsley; its seeds are tiny, ridged, and oval, looking like celery seeds, and range from light brown to grayish-green in color.

The seeds smell faintly of thyme; the fragrance becomes stronger if they are crushed. They are pungent, peppery, and slightly bitter, with a taste like thyme, but stronger, and undertones of cumin, another relative, and they leave a lingering numbing sensation on the tongue if chewed. Their flavor mellows slightly when they are cooked. Like thyme, ajowan seeds contain high levels of the volatile oil thymol, and ajowan is mainly grown for that essential oil, which has a variety of medicinal uses, as it is both a germicide and an antiseptic.

Ajowan seeds are most commonly sold whole but are occa-

(continued on next page)

sionally available ground. They are so small that grinding is usually unnecessary, but if desired, this can be done at home with a mortar and pestle or spice grinder.

Ajowan pairs well with starchy foods like potatoes and root vegetables, legumes, and beans. In India, it is often added to dishes made with lentils and other legumes for its digestive properties as much as for its flavor. It is also used in flatbreads like rotis and in fritters and other deep-fried foods. It features prominently in the vegetarian dishes of the' Gujarat region, and it is an ingredient in many curry blends, especially for fish and vegetable curries, and in the Ethiopian spice mix berbere (see page 31). It is also added to chutneys and many pickles. Because of its strong flavor, ajowan should be used sparingly so it won't overwhelm other flavors; a healthy pinch is enough to flavor a pot of rice or steamed cabbage. A mix of crushed ajowan, cumin, and coriander seeds makes a good seasoning for grilled chicken and fish.

MEDICINAL USES: Ajowan seeds are chewed as a digestive and to relieve intestinal distress, and ajowan tea (see sidebar) has long been used to treat indigestion. Ajowan is important in Ayurvedic medicine, and it is viewed as a powerful cleanser of the body. Traditionally, ajowan was prescribed to cure cholera and asthma. It is also believed to soothe colic.

AJOWAN TEA Toast

1 teaspoon ajowan seeds and 1 teaspoon cumin seeds together in a small skillet. Combine with 1 cup water in a small saucepan and bring to a boil. Strain and sweeten with sugar to taste.

Spices and dried herbs should be stored in a cool place (ideally, not in a decorative spice rack above your stove) away from direct sunlight. Seeds that are rich in oil, such as sesame seeds and poppy seeds, are best stored in the freezer for longer periods, as their high oil content means they can turn rancid quickly.

As a general rule, ground spices are best used within six months to a year, though some will retain their pungency longer—uncap the jar and sniff for freshness. Whole spices keep for much longer, at least a year and often for several years. Dried herbs should be used within six months or so— old dried herbs smell like dried hay.

Spice purveyors who sell their spices in bulk or large quantities (as well as other online sources) often also offer sets of sturdy glass jars with tight-fitting lids. If you buy spices in bulk, these can be a good investment, as they will keep your spices fresher for longer.

ALEPPO CHILE

See Red Pepper Flakes, page 77.

ALLSPICE

BOTANICAL NAMES: *Pimenta officinalis, P. dioica*
OTHER NAMES: Jamaica pepper, myrtle pepper, pimento
FORMS: whole berries and ground

Allspice berries are the fruit of a tall tropical evergreen tree in the myrtle family. It is native to the West Indies; some sources believe it is also indigenous to parts of Latin America. Its Spanish name, *pimenta,* means "pepper," because the early Spanish explorers, who were seeking the Spice Islands, thought they had reached their destination and mistook the berries for peppercorns. Today, allspice is primarily grown in Jamaica, the Caribbean, and South America; the best is said to come from Jamaica.

ALLSPICE TEA Pour 1 cup boiling water over 1 to 2 teaspoons ground allspice and let steep for 10 to 20 minutes before drinking.

Allspice berries are still harvested by hand. They are picked when they are green and immature and then either sun-dried for up to ten days or commercially dried. When properly dried, the berries turn reddish-brown to purple-brown. Their rough surface conceals tiny seeds that rattle slightly when the berries are shaken (shaking the dried berries to see if the seeds rattle is the traditional way of determining whether they are dry enough). The outer "shells" actually have more flavor than the seeds themselves.

Allspice berries are faintly aromatic, but the flavor is pungent when they are ground. The berries are easy to grind, and it is best to buy them whole and grind them with a mortar and pestle or in a spice grinder as needed. Ground allspice is a rich, warm brown, and the taste is like that of a combination of spices—

cinnamon, nutmeg or mace, and cloves, with peppery overtones—hence the name allspice. Some people, in fact, mistakenly believe that ground allspice is a spice blend rather than a single spice.

Allspice is widely used in the cooking of the West Indies and the Caribbean, most notably in Jamaican jerk seasoning (see page 151) for grilled chicken. In North America and Europe, allspice is most often an ingredient in cakes, cookies, and other baked goods and sweets. It is found in rich curries in northern India and in Middle Eastern stews and North African dishes such as tagines. It also seasons pâtés and sausages. Allspice is used as a pickling spice in many cuisines; in Scandinavia, pickled herring is made with allspice. The whole berries often flavor mulled wine or other hot drinks, as well as the liquid used to poach fruits such as pears. Allspice complements sweet spices like nutmeg and cinnamon, and it is an ingredient in apple pie and pumpkin pie spice blends. It is also important in the food industry, in ketchups, preserved meats, and some canned fish.

MEDICINAL USES: Allspice has traditionally been used to relieve stomachaches and other digestive problems. Folk medicine also prescribes it for toothaches, rheumatism, and a variety of other ailments, and it can be used to make a soothing tea (see sidebar).

AMCHUR

BOTANICAL NAME: *Mangifera indica*
OTHER NAMES: amchoor, aamchur, dried mango powder
FORMS: whole dried slices and ground

Amchur is dried green mango, most often seen as a powder but also sold as whole dried mango slices. The fruit is picked unripe, peeled, sliced, and sun-dried. Mango trees are native to India (in Hindi, *am* means "mango" and *choor* means "powder"), Burma, and Malaysia; they have grown in India for more than four thousand years.

The dried slices are light brown and the powder is pale tan or beige. Occasionally, turmeric is added to the powder, which gives it a yellowish hue. Amchur has a warm, fruity fragrance and an acidic, tart taste, with a slight fruitiness. It pairs well with vegetables such as cauliflower, eggplant, and potatoes and with legumes such as chickpeas. In India, it is used in potato fillings for samosas, *pakoras,* and other savory pastries, and in curries, soups, stews, lentil and vegetable dishes, chutneys, and pickles; whole slices are sometimes added to lentil and vegetable dishes. Amchur combines well with other spices such as cloves, coriander, and cumin, as well as ginger and chiles, and it is a key ingredient in the spice blend chaat masala (see page 52).

Amchur is used as both a souring agent and as a meat tenderizer. It gives food a tart, tangy, sour taste without adding moisture, and it can be substituted for lemon juice in many dishes; use 1 teaspoon amchur powder in place of 3 tablespoons lemon juice. It sometimes stands in for tamarind as a souring agent. Like papayas, mangoes contain an enzyme that helps tenderize foods, so amchur is used in many marinades, particularly for meats and poultry that will be grilled or cooked in a tandoor oven.

ANARDANA

BOTANICAL NAME: *Punica granatum*
FORMS: whole seeds and ground

Anardana is dried wild pomegranate seeds. Wild pomegranate grows in northern India, Jammu, and Kashmir; Iran; and the southern Himalayas. The seeds, with the pulp surrounding them, are slowly air-dried and then used whole or ground.

The whole dried seeds are dark red to almost black, sticky, and somewhat jammy, with a hard pale seed in the center, and they tend to clump together. They have an acidic, slightly fruity taste. The medium-fine powder is reddish-brown and has a very fruity, slightly sour aroma and a subtle, slightly dry, sour-sweet flavor. For most dishes, the whole seeds should be dry-roasted in a skillet and then ground to a coarse or fine powder as desired.

Anardana is widely used as a souring agent in Iran and in India, particularly in northern Indian and Punjabi cuisines. With its tart, fruity flavor, it's also a good alternative to tamarind. In India, it adds acidic tang to chutneys, relishes, and spice rubs for meat and seafood, as well as to lentil and rice dishes, braises, and certain Moghul-style preparations. Its unique flavor pairs well with herbs such as cilantro and mint. In the Middle East, anardana is used for breads and some pastries. The coarsely ground (or whole) seeds can be sprinkled over vegetable dishes or salads, including fruit salads.

MEDICINAL USES: Anardana is believed to help digestion and is used in Ayurvedic preparations for various ailments. It is high in vitamin C and potassium.

The traditional way of grinding spices is with a mortar and pestle, used in cultures around the world from Southeast Asia to Italy and Africa to Latin America. At its most basic, a mortar and pestle consist of a bowl-shaped container with what looks like a small club for grinding the ingredients. They may be made of marble, glass or porcelain, hardwood, or stoneware. Larger ones, with a mortar about 6 inches in diameter, are more useful than the small ones found in most gourmet shops.

The Mexican version of a mortar, called a *molcajete* (the Spanish word for "pestle" is *tejolete*), is made of basalt (volcanic rock) and stands on three legs. Some cooks outside of Mexico find it preferable to a regular mortar because its rough surface makes grinding easier and more efficient. (A *molcajete* should be "cured" by grinding away the roughest surfaces before it is used for the first time: Grind raw rice or coarse salt a handful at a time until it remains white rather than turning grayish. Then rinse the *molcajete* and *tejolete* thoroughly and dry them.)

Today, the easiest way to grind spices is with an electric coffee grinder (and these are now sometimes marketed as spice grinders). It is efficient and makes quick work of the task. Depending on the type and number of spices you are grinding, it may be more effective to grind them separately rather than together; grind hard spices such as coriander seeds first, then add softer spices such as cumin seeds. If you need a large amount of freshly ground black pepper—for *spaghetti cacio e pepe*, for example—try grinding it in a spice grinder rather than a pepper mill; the fragrance will be intoxicating. It's really best to have a separate grinder reserved for spices, but if you do use the same grinder for both coffee and spices, clean it thoroughly—or grind some raw rice in it and then wipe it out—after grinding spices so that your next cup of coffee doesn't taste like coriander.

Some recipes call for cracked or crushed peppercorns, cardamom pods, or other spices. You can pulse these in a spice grinder, but a better way is to crush them under a heavy skillet, or pound them with a rolling pin. (If you put them on a kitchen towel, they are less likely to hop all over the counter— or put them in a heavy-duty plastic bag.) Of course, you can also use a mortar and pestle.

ANISE

BOTANICAL NAME: *Pimpinella anisum*
OTHER NAMES: aniseed, sweet cumin, saunf
FORMS: whole seeds and ground

Aniseeds, native to the Middle East, are one of the oldest-known spices. The plant is a delicate annual related to caraway, cumin, dill, and fennel. In fact, in India, both fennel seeds and aniseeds are called *saunf* because they resemble each other so closely. Anise is now grown in Turkey, India, Spain, North Africa, Greece, Mexico, Central America, and other temperate regions.

The small, oval, crescent-shaped ridged seeds are actually the split halves of what are called the plant's fruits. They range in color from pale brown to greenish-gray, and they often have

(continued on next page)

a bit of the fine stalk that is found in the center of the fruits still attached. They are sweet and aromatic, with a distinct licorice flavor and taste. Ground anise is a warm brown color. Aniseeds are best bought whole rather than ground, as the spice quickly loses its fragrance and flavor once ground. Look for seeds with a minimal amount of stalks and husks. If you are grinding the seeds at home rather than using them whole, toasting them first in a dry skillet will make them slightly brittle and easier to grind or crush.

Aniseeds pair especially well with fish and seafood and poultry. They enhance the flavor of stews, particularly beef, and are used in many other savory dishes, often in combination with dill, fennel, and/or coriander seeds. Anise is a popular seasoning both in India, where it is used in many seafood and vegetable dishes and in curries, and in Morocco. It is used in breads and other baked goods, including cakes and cookies, in Scandinavia (think rye bread), Germany, Italy, and other European countries. In India, the seeds are "bloomed" in hot oil and used as a finishing garnish for vegetable and lentil dishes.

The seeds have long been considered a digestive, and the raw or lightly toasted, or, occasionally, sweetened or candy-coated, seeds can be chewed as a breath freshener after meals. Anise is the base of many licorice-flavored aperitifs and liqueurs, including ouzo in Greece, pastis in France, sambuca in Italy, arrack in the

---

ANISE TEA Anise tea is believed to aid in digestion, relieve stomach cramps, and stimulate the appetite. Pour 1 cup boiling water over 1 teaspoon crushed aniseeds and steep for 10 to 15 minutes; strain before drinking.

eastern Mediterranean, and anisette in many countries. It is also widely used in confectionery.

MEDICINAL USES: In addition to their use as a breath freshener and digestive, aniseeds are believed to ease stomach cramps and help prevent flatulence (see sidebar, opposite). In Ayurdevic medicine, aniseeds are used to treat bronchial ailments, colds, and coughs.

ANNATTO

BOTANICAL NAME: *Bixa orellana*
OTHER NAMES: achiote
FORMS: whole seeds and ground

Achiote is the Mexican name for what are often called annatto seeds in the United States and elsewhere. They come from a small evergreen tree that is native to Mexico, the Caribbean, and Central and South America. The tree's heart-shaped red or brown seedpods are filled with small, hard, triangular seeds surrounded by reddish pulp. After being harvested, the seeds are cleaned and dried. They have a peppery, slightly bittersweet fragrance and a mild, musky flavor. Look for annatto seeds that are brick-red in color, not brownish. The seeds keep almost indefinitely.

Annatto is widely used as a dye and as a natural coloring agent for many foods, including cheeses such as Muenster and Leicester, margarine, butter, and cooking oils. In the kitchen, the seeds, in various forms, are also primarily used as a coloring agent, rather than as a seasoning.

In Mexico, the seeds are usually ground into a seasoning paste. In Oaxaca and Chiapas, the paste is pure ground seeds; in the Yu-

(continued on next page)

catán, it contains other spices and flavorings such as cumin and coriander seeds, black peppercorns, oregano, and garlic, and it is called *recado rojo* (*rojo* means "red," and *recado* refers to a mixture of spices). *Recado rojo* is used to season chicken, pork, and fish, as well as tamales, that will be baked in banana leaves, and it is also added to soups and stews. Oil infused with annatto seeds (see sidebar) will add color and a mild flavor to many dishes. Annatto is used in one form or another, including the ground seeds, throughout the Caribbean and Latin America, and it is an ingredient in many Filipino dishes.

ANNATTO OIL Combine ¼ cup annatto seeds and 2 cups canola or other neutral oil in a saucepan and heat over medium heat just until small bubbles form around the seeds; do not overheat, or the oil can turn bitter. Remove from the heat and let cool completely, then strain the oil and store in the refrigerator.

MEDICINAL USES: Annatto can be used to relieve heartburn and stomach distress. In certain cultures, it is believed to improve liver function and lower cholesterol.

ARMENIAN SPICE MIX

OTHER NAMES: chaimen

Chaimen means "fenugreek" in Armenian, and that is one of the main ingredients in this versatile blend. It usually also contains paprika, cumin, cayenne, and garlic; allspice is often an ingredient as well. Chaimen is used to season *basturma,* the spicy Armenian air-dried cured beef. It is also added to soups, stews, and meat or vegetable dishes. And it can be mixed with olive oil (or even just water) or yogurt to make a delicious dip for flatbreads or vegetables.

ASAFOETIDA

BOTANICAL NAME: *Ferula asafoetida*
OTHER NAMES: asafetida, hing, stinking gum, devil's dung
FORMS: blocks, granules, and ground

Asafoetida is not, in fact, a spice, although it is treated like one in Indian cooking. It is actually the dried resin, or latex, extracted from several species of ferula, or giant fennel, a tall perennial plant. Some varieties of ferula are poisonous; the plants that produce asafoetida are found primarily in Iran, in Afghanistan, and in Kashmir in India. The plant has a distinctive smell, and the aroma of asafoetida is pungent, slightly sulfurous, and very unpleasant—hence some of its more colorful common names (listed above). When it is cooked in small quantities with other ingredients, however, its flavor mellows.

The latex is harvested from incisions made in the roots of the ferula plants over a period of time; the process of gathering the milky liquid can take up to several months. The hardened latex is collected and further processed into various forms. Blocks of asafoetida are initially a pale creamy color but darken to reddish and then reddish-brown as they age. Asafoetida is also sold in granules or as a powder, which is the easiest form to use. The tan or brown powder is usually mixed with a starch such as wheat flour or rice flour for ease of use; the rice flour version is generally considered of better quality. Turmeric is sometimes added as a coloring agent, giving the powder a yellowish hue. In any case, asafoetida should

(continued on next page)

always be stored in a tightly sealed container because of its off-putting aroma.

Asafoetida is used primarily in Indian cooking. The powder should generally be fried in oil before it is added to the main ingredients; other spices may be added along with it, though when mustard seeds are used, they are fried in the oil first. Other complementary spices and aromatics include cumin seeds, curry leaves, dried chiles, ginger, and garlic. (Asafoetida is one of the ingredients in chaat masala; see page 52.) A pinch or two of asafoetida is enough to flavor a pot of lentils or chickpeas or of vegetables such as potatoes, cauliflower, onions, peas, or quick-cooking greens; it is added to many vegetarian dishes. It also seasons fish curries and various pickles. Some have likened the aroma and flavor of asafoetida to those of pickled or even fermented garlic, and in India, Brahmins and Jains, who do not eat garlic, turn to asafoetida as a substitute. It adds a pungent, slightly fermented and sulfuric flavor that is akin to but much lighter than that of garlic or other alliums.

MEDICINAL USES: In India, asafoetida is prescribed for bronchitis and other respiratory problems; it is also believed to prevent flatulence (hence its inclusion in many dishes made with beans, lentils, and other legumes).

[B]

BAHARAT

Baharat is a Middle Eastern spice blend that is sometimes called seven-spice mix, although both the number and spices can vary from country to country. The word *baharat* means "spices" in Arabic, but it also refers to this popular mix of aromatic spices. A classic blend includes cumin, coriander, cinnamon, cloves, nutmeg, cardamom, and black pepper, but many versions also include paprika and/or chile powder; in Turkey, dried mint is often added, and dried rose petals appear in some North African blends. Sumac and saffron are other possible regional additions. An all-purpose blend, baharat adds deep flavor, sweet and spicy notes, and a rich color to a variety of dishes. It is used to season rice dishes, including pilafs, and is stirred into soups, stews, and sauces. It also makes an excellent rub for grilled or slow-simmered meats, especially lamb, and grilled fish, and it seasons ground meat for kebabs. Baharat is blended with oil and used as a marinade, and it can also be combined with oil, and perhaps garlic and herbs, to make a table condiment.

BAHARAT
cinnamon, cardamom , black peppercorns, nutmeg, coriander, cloves, and cumin

BARBERRY

BOTANICAL NAME: *Berberis vulgaris*

OTHER NAMES: thornberries, zereshk

FORMS: whole berries

Various species of the barberry bush are native to Central Asia, North Africa, and parts of Europe, where it grows wild. There are many different varieties, and some of the shrubs are considered purely decorative—the fruits of some barberries can be toxic, and only *B. vulgaris* should be used in cooking. (The branches of some species have thorns; the name "thornberries" derives from the belief that barberry leaves were part of Christ's crown of thorns.) The small oval berries turn bright red when ripe and are harvested then.

Barberries are very tart when fresh (they were traditionally used as a souring agent), and so, especially in the Middle East, are more often dried for culinary purposes. When dried, the berries look like small dried currants. They should be soft, moist, and deep red; avoid dried barberries that have darkened, a sign of age. Their fruity flavor is tart-sweet, and they can be eaten as a snack, like dried cranberries.

Barberries are called *zereshk* in Iran, and *zereshk polo* is a favorite version of that classic Persian rice dish. They are also essential in the celebratory wedding dish known as "jeweled rice." Barberries can be incorporated into a spice rub for grilled lamb or game meats, and they can be made into a jelly or jam to be served with mutton or other fatty meats. Barberries are used in rice dishes in Afghanistan. Be sure to remove any errant stems when rinsing or soaking barberries in cold water. In Persian mythology, they are considered a "cold" food; "hot-natured" people are encouraged to eat "cold" foods to achieve balance.

MEDICINAL USES: Barberries are high in vitamin C and antioxidants; some consider them a superfood.

BASIL

BOTANICAL NAMES: *Ocimum basilicum* (sweet basil); *O. sanctum* (holy basil)
FORMS: fresh and dried leaves

Basil, a member of the mint family, is native to India, where it has long been considered a sacred herb; if not also indigenous to Iran and Africa, it has grown there for so long that its origins are lost in the mists of time. Sweet basil is the most common culinary type today, but there are many subspecies and hybrids. A sweet basil plant can be as tall as 2 feet or more; it has dark green, smooth, oval leaves and is strongly aromatic, with an herbaceous, anise-like fragrance and undertones of mint; the leaves have a peppery anise taste, again with notes of mint as well as of cloves. The leaves of holy basil, the variety known in India, have jagged edges and can range in color from dark green to purple. There are several different types, including some with a peppery, minty taste, perhaps with hints of ginger, and others with a more citrusy taste; *tulsi* is the Indian name. Opal basil has dark purple leaves and often a spicier flavor than sweet basil; purple ruffle basil has crinkled purple leaves with ruffled edges and tastes very similar to sweet basil. Other varieties include lemon basil and cinnamon basil, their names reflecting their flavors. Dried basil is usually sweet basil; high-quality dried basil is dark green and has a delicate minty, peppery flavor.

Basil complements most summer vegetables, from zucchini to eggplant, but probably none more so than tomatoes, whether

(continued on page 29)

BASIL
dried and fresh

sliced ripe tomatoes or a quick-simmered tomato sauce. (If you have only dried basil, crumble it into a tablespoon or so of olive oil and let it infuse briefly, then drizzle that over your sliced tomatoes.) It is a favorite herb throughout the Mediterranean, particularly in Italy, where one of its most famous incarnations is in pesto, the pounded sauce of basil, garlic, olive oil, pine nuts, and Parmigiano-Reggiano. Pesto is used as a pasta sauce, of course, but it is also excellent as a fresh condiment served with grilled fish, or simply spread on grilled bread for crostini. The French version of pesto, *pistou,* is the classic garnish for minestrone. In India, basil is used more often in drinks than in savory dishes; it is also valued for its medicinal purposes. Purple and opal basil, as well as holy basil, are used in Southeast Asian cooking, in soups, stir-fries, and other dishes. The spicier basils are also popular in this region. Finally, basil also has a place in sweet dishes. Basil sorbet is very refreshing, and fruits such as sliced strawberries or blueberries can be macerated with sugar and slivered basil. Panna cotta and delicate custards can be infused with basil, and it adds a lovely note to poached peaches or rhubarb.

Note: In India, sweet basil seeds, called *subja,* are used in drinks and desserts. When soaked in water, the tiny black seeds swell and develop a translucent gelatinous coating. They are the basis of *falooda,* a sweet, milky drink flavored with rose cordial that can be served as dessert (they are sometimes referred to as falooda seeds). They are also used as a garnish for desserts such as *kulfi,* Indian ice cream.

BAY LEAVES

BOTANICAL NAMES: *Laurelus nobilis* (Turkish); *Umbellularia californica* (Californian)
OTHER NAMES: bay laurel, sweet laurel, sweet bay (Turkish)
FORMS: fresh and dried

The bay laurel is a tall evergreen tree native to Asia Minor, but it has grown around the Mediterranean for centuries and has long been associated with the cuisines of the region. Its Latin name means "noble laurel," and in Greek and Roman times, winners of battles or sports competitions were often crowned with a laurel wreath. Poets were sometimes recognized in the same fashion— thus the origin of the term *poet laureate*. Most bay leaves, including those on the supermarket spice shelf, come from Turkey. California bay leaves are from an entirely different species and are much stronger than Turkish bay leaves.

Unlike most herbs, bay leaves are traditionally preferable when dried, although recently, more chefs have begun using the fresh leaves. The fresh leaves can be strong and bitter, but they mellow somewhat when dried. Both types of bay leaves smell like a combination of menthol and eucalyptus, with notes of camphor. Look for deep green leaves when buying dried bay; pale or yellow leaves are older or were improperly stored and will have less fragrance. California bay leaves are longer and narrower than bay laurel leaves. Cookbook recipes that do not specify the particular type of bay leaf should be assumed to mean Turkish leaves; if substituting California bay, use half the amount.

Bay leaves pair well with other Mediterranean herbs such as rosemary, marjoram, oregano, sage, savory, and thyme. They are at their best in stews, braises, and other long-simmered dishes.

Moroccan tagines often include bay leaves, and in Turkey, they are used to season lamb and rice dishes, including pilafs. They complement tomatoes well and are added to many tomato sauces. Bay leaves are an essential seasoning in bouillabaisse and many other Mediterranean fish dishes. The leaves are usually added whole and then removed before serving, but they can also be crumbled before being added to long-cooked stews and the like. Bay leaves are often an ingredient in rubs for steak and other meats, and they are an essential part of a bouquet garni (see page 36). They should not be eaten whole.

BENGALI FIVE-SPICE MIX

See Panch Phoron.

BENNE SEEDS

See Sesame.

BERBERE

Berbere is a spicy Ethiopian seasoning mix that typically contains ajowan, cayenne or other chile powder, paprika, fenugreek, cardamom, coriander, cumin, cinnamon, cloves, and ginger, but regional variations are also made with nutmeg and other ingredients. Like garam masala in Indian cuisine, it has broad applications, and local cooks tend to tailor it to the preparation at hand. Most versions have a coarse, earthy texture and a brick-red color. Berbere is an essential ingredient in *doro wat,* the chicken stew that is considered Ethiopia's national dish, and it adds its pungent flavor to other stews and to soups. It is used as a dry rub for meats,

(continued on next page)

poultry, and fish that will be grilled, roasted, or panfried. Berbere can be combined with oil to make a seasoning paste, or a dip for flatbreads, and it is often fried in oil at the start of cooking to provide the seasoning base for a stew or other dish.

BLACK CARDAMOM

See Cardamom.

BLACK CUMIN

See Cumin.

BLACK LEMON

See Black Lime.

BLACK LIME

BOTANICAL NAME: *Citrus latifolia*
OTHER NAMES: dried lime, black lemon, loomi, omani limes, noomi basra
FORMS: whole and ground

Limes, like all citrus fruits, are native to Southeast Asia, but dried limes come from the Arabian Peninsula. They are Persian limes, and they were originally dried on the trees themselves. Today, they are picked when ripe and dried in the sun; sometimes they are boiled before drying.

Dried limes are about 1 inch in diameter and range in color

(continued on page 34)

from off-white to tan to black. They have a faint citrus fragrance and a sharp, sour flavor, with a slightly fermented taste. As they dry, most of the pulp dissolves, leaving a hard outer shell. Dried limes are sold both whole and powdered; if possible, buy whole limes and crack or crush or grind them at home, for more intense flavor. Wrap them in a towel and hit them with a mallet or hammer to crack them. They are quite brittle and, once split, can be ground with a mortar and pestle or in a spice grinder. Make sure to remove any seeds from the shell before grinding. Commercial powdered lime is somewhat coarse.

Dried limes are used in Persian cooking as a souring agent, like tamarind. They are usually cracked or ground before they are added to a dish but are occasionally left whole. If adding a whole dried lime or two to a stew or soup, carefully pierce it with a sharp skewer or knife to allow the cooking liquid to permeate it and absorb the flavor of the lime—and be sure to squeeze the aromatic juices from the lime back into the stew at the end of cooking. Fish is cooked with black lime throughout the Persian Gulf, and powdered black lime flavors pilafs and other rice dishes; it can also be used as a rub for grilled fish, poultry, and meat. Black lime is occasionally one of the ingredients in local versions of the Middle Eastern spice mix baharat (see page 24).

BLACK ONION SEEDS

See Nigella.

BORAGE

BOTANICAL NAME: *Borago officinalis*
OTHER NAMES: bee bread, starflower
FORMS: fresh and dried leaves

Borage is native to the Middle East, specifically Persia and modern-day Turkey. It has droopy green leaves and purple or blue star-shaped flowers and is as widely grown as an ornamental plant as for culinary use. Both the leaves and flowers have a distinct cucumber-like taste, and borage is often used in refreshing summer drinks; it is also one of the ingredients in Pimm's Cup, the popular British cocktail. The dried flowers are infused to make a soothing tea in Iran, where borage is known as *gol gavzaban* (spellings vary), and elsewhere in the Middle East, as well as throughout Europe.

BOUQUET GARNI

A bouquet garni is a bundle of herbs used in classic French cooking to season stocks, soups, and stews. The basic composition is 3 parsley sprigs or stems, 1 thyme sprig, and 1 bay leaf (large pots of stock or broth, of course, need larger bouquets), which are tied together with kitchen twine or wrapped in cheesecloth for easy removal at the end of cooking; sometimes the herbs are instead wrapped in a leek green or a celery stalk. Although a bouquet garni is easy to put together with ingredients that are usually on hand, dried herb blends of the same ingredients are available from some specialty shops and spice merchants. These are sold in jars or packaged like tea bags.

CARAWAY

BOTANICAL NAME: *Carum carvi*
OTHER NAMES: siya jeera, Persian caraway, Roman cumin, wild cumin; shahi jeera, sajira (black caraway)
FORMS: whole seeds and ground

Caraway is a biennial herb native to Asia and northern and central Europe. A member of the same family as parsley, it is an ancient plant, and evidence of its culinary use dates back to 3000 BC. Today, the Netherlands is the largest producer; caraway is also grown in Scandinavia, Germany, Poland, Russia, Canada, the United States, Morocco, and northern India.

The small, ridged, curved brown seeds—the split halves of the plant's fruits—are pointed at the ends. They have a warm, very pungent aroma that is like a combination of the aromas of dill and aniseed and a tangy, nutty flavor. Black caraway seeds are darker and thinner and they have a flavor of cumin that is not found in regular caraway; in fact, they are sometimes referred to, erroneously, as black cumin. Both caraway and cumin may be called *jeera* or *zira* in India; adding to the confusion is the fact that the Swedish name for caraway is *kummin*.

CARAWAY TEA Add 1 to 2 teaspoons crushed caraway seeds to 1 cup boiling water and steep for 10 to 15 minutes, then strain.

Caraway is harvested in the early morning, when the dew is still on the plants—once dried by the sun's warmth, the seedpods will shatter, dispersing the precious seeds onto the ground below. The plant stalks are allowed to dry and further ripen for about ten days, then threshed to remove the seeds. Ground caraway loses its fragrance fairly quickly, so it's best to purchase whole seeds, which are easy to grind if first toasted in a dry skillet.

Caraway is used predominantly in Europe and the Middle East. It pairs well with cabbage (notably in sauerkraut), fruits such as apples, and pork. It seasons myriad sausages, and it is found in many European cheeses. Caraway seeds are used in European breads such as rye bread and the French *pain d'épices*. They are also found in some versions of the spice blends ras el hanout, garam masala, and harissa (see pages 248, 131, and 143). In the Middle East, a dish made with caraway called *moughli* is served to celebrate childbirth. Black caraway, which is native to Persia, is used in northern India, Pakistan, and Bangladesh, where it adds its distinctive rich, nutty taste to biryanis, kormas, and some Moghul-style and tandoori preparations. Caraway's essential oil flavors liqueurs such as aquavit, kümmel, and schnapps.

MEDICINAL USES: Considered a digestive, caraway can be used to make a soothing tea (see sidebar). The seeds, though bitter, can be chewed (preferably after being toasted) to relieve an upset stomach.

CARAWAY

43

Toasting spices brings out their flavor and fragrance. The easiest way to do this is to dry-roast them in a cast-iron or other heavy skillet: Heat the pan for a minute or two over medium heat, then add the spices and toast, shaking the pan frequently to prevent scorching, for 2 to 3 minutes, or until very aromatic; depending on the spices, they may turn a few shades darker. Immediately transfer the spices to a plate or bowl to cool, so they don't burn in the hot skillet. It is best to toast spices whole and then grind or crush them if desired; ground spices will toast unevenly and are much more likely to burn.

CARDAMOM

BOTANICAL NAME: *Elettaria cardamomum*
OTHER NAMES: green cardamom (see below for brown and red cardamom)
FORMS: pods, whole seeds, and ground

Cardamom is a tropical perennial bush in the ginger family native to southern India and Sri Lanka. It is also grown in Vietnam, Guatemala, and Tanzania. It is one of the most expensive spices in the world, a fact explained in part by its relatively limited growing area and the laborious harvesting process. Cardamom is called the queen of spices in India (pepper is the king), and the best green cardamom comes from Kerala.

(continued on page 46)

CARDAMOM
Chinese black cardamom and green cardamom

Cardamom is harvested by hand just before the fruit is ripe—if left to mature, the pods will split open and the seeds will be scattered and lost. Because the pods do not all ripen at the same time, harvesting takes place over several months, with skilled workers choosing only those pods that are ready. The best cardamom is dried in special sheds heated by wood-fired furnaces rather than under the hot sun, which would bleach the pods.

Green cardamom pods are about half an inch long and contain twelve to twenty dark brown to black seeds that may be oily or somewhat sticky. Cardamom has a warm, sweet fragrance with delicate citrus and floral top notes and a refreshing undertone of eucalyptus. The seeds are aromatic, with a floral scent and a fresh, lemony flavor. Look for bright green pods. White cardamom pods have been bleached and should generally be avoided, although white cardamom is used in some Indian desserts where the green color would be undesirable. When used whole, the pods are usually cracked before being added to a stew or other dish. Some recipes call for the whole seeds, but they are more often ground; the seeds are best ground in a spice grinder. If buying ground cardamom, note that it should be a fairly dark brown; lighter powders are made from ground whole pods and are of lesser quality, as the husks have little flavor.

Cardamom is used in a wide variety of savory and sweet preparations. It features prominently in Indian, Persian, Turkish, and Arabic cuisines, in stews, curries, and biryanis and other rice dishes; it is also used to season vegetables. It is an essential ingredient in garam masala (see page 131), and it is found in many other spice blends as well, including baharat and ras el hanout (see pages 24 and 248), and in curry powders. It flavors many Indian sweets and desserts, including *kulfi* and rice pudding, and it complements poached pears and other fruits. Cardamom pairs well with sweet spices such as cinnamon, allspice, cloves, and nutmeg, and in Scandinavia, it is used in cakes, cookies, and Danish pastries. In the Middle East and North Africa, cardamom often flavors the coffee served after a meal; it is also added to tea. Since cardamom is a stimulant, it was used in love potions in mythology.

Black cardamom (sp. *Amomum subulatum*), also called brown cardamom, is not true cardamom; its many common names include bastard cardamom and false cardamom. Also known as Bengal cardamom, Nepal cardamom, and winged cardamom, it is valued for certain preparations. The dried oval pods, which are much larger than those of regular cardamom, are dark brown, ribbed, and rough, and they can contain as many as fifty seeds. The pods have a smoky, woody aroma, and the seeds have a camphorous fragrance and taste, with slightly sweet notes. Black cardamom is used whole, usually crushed, or finely or coarsely ground in certain Indian meat and vegetable dishes, especially more rustic or spicier preparations.

Chinese black cardamom (sp. *Amomum costatum*), also known as red cardamom, is a different species, grown in southwestern China and in Thailand. The large dark-reddish-brown pods, which can be 1 inch long or more, are ribbed and sometimes still have the stems intact. They have a strong, spicy flavor and, unless dried in the sun, a gentle smoky flavor from the drying process. Chinese black cardamom is popular in Szechuan and other Chinese regional cuisines and in Vietnamese cooking. The hard pods are added whole to slow-cooked dishes, such as braises, and to steamed rice or soups. The ground seeds are sometimes added to stir-fries.

CAROM/CARUM

See Ajowan.

CASSIA

BOTANICAL NAMES: *Cinnamomum cassia* (Chinese), *C. burmannii* (Indonesian), *C. louririi* (Vietnamese), *C. tamala* (Indian)
OTHER NAMES: false cinnamon
FORMS: sticks, pieces, and ground

Cassia comes from the bark of a tropical evergreen that is related to the bay laurel tree. It is native to Indonesia and, according to some sources, also to northeastern India. The *Cinnamomum* family includes dozens of members; *C. zeylanicum* is considered "true cinnamon" (see Cinnamon, page 83). Like cinnamon, cassia is an ancient spice, and its history dates back centuries. It has been cultivated in China since 4000 BC, and it was an important part of the spice trade. The major producers of cassia today are Indonesia, China, and Vietnam; it is cultivated in India, too, where the leaves of the tree are also used as a spice (see Cassia Leaves, page 50).

Cassia is harvested at the beginning of the rainy season, when it is easiest to remove the bark from the trees. The bark is cut off in large sections; depending on the region, the coarser outer bark may be scraped off before the cassia is dried in the sun. As it dries, the bark, which is thicker than cinnamon bark, curls into what are called quills; cassia is also sometimes sold as small flat pieces. Once dried, cassia turns a dark reddish-brown; its color is darker than that of cinnamon. Although the quills, or sticks, can be used whole, the bark is very hard and difficult to grind at home, so much of the crop is ground commercially. Ground cassia is also darker and redder than ground cinnamon. Cassia has a warm, sweet fragrance similar to that of cinnamon but less intense; the flavor is stronger than that of cinnamon, mildly sweet but with a bitter undertone. Saigon, or Vietnamese, cassia has a higher oil content and a more pungent taste than the other cassias on the market.

Although it is illegal to label cassia as "cinnamon" in some countries, no such distinctions are made in the United States, and in fact, the cinnamon found in almost all supermarkets is actually cassia, most of which comes from Indonesia. In North America, cassia cinnamon is a favorite ingredient in cookies, spice cakes, and other baked goods and desserts. In many other countries, however, it is more widely used in savory dishes. In India, cassia—often as whole quills—seasons curries, rice, and vegetables. In Malaysia and Southeast Asia, it is used in savory stews and rice dishes. Cassia is also one of the ingredients in Chinese five-spice powder (see page 79) and the Middle Eastern seven-spice mix (see Baharat, page 24).

MEDICINAL USES: Cassia has been used in traditional medicine to treat a variety of ailments, including stomachaches and other digestive problems. It is considered an appetite stimulant and is valued for its antioxidant properties.

CASSIA LEAVES

BOTANICAL NAME: *Cinnamomum tamala*

OTHER NAMES: Indian bay leaves, tej patta, tejpat

FORMS: fresh and dried

Cassia leaves come from the tree, native to northern India, that is the source of cassia cinnamon (see Cassia, page 48); it is in the same family as the species that is the source of our familiar bay leaves. The shiny dark green leaves are much larger than bay leaves and each one has three prominent veins running down its length, rather than the single vein of bay leaves. The aroma and taste are mildly cinnamony, with a hint of cloves. Cassia leaves are widely used in Indian cooking and in some Asian cuisines, more often dried than fresh. They are added to Indian curries, stews, and rice dishes and to Moghul-style biryanis, kormas, and vegetable pulaos. The leaves are also used in Kashmiri and Nepalese cooking, and they are infused to make an herbal tea in Kashmir. Cassia leaves are one of the ingredients in garam masala (see page 131).

MEDICINAL USES: Traditional medicine ascribes antibacterial, antifungal, and anti-inflammatory properties to cassia leaves. An infusion of cassia leaves is sometimes prescribed for an upset stomach and other digestive disorders.

CELERY SEEDS

BOTANICAL NAME: *Apium graveolens*
OTHER NAMES: wild celery, smallage
FORMS: whole and ground

Native to eastern and southern Europe, the celery plant that supplies the familiar seeds is a descendant of wild celery, or smallage, which was used for medicinal purposes in ancient times. Related to parsley, it's a biennial that is now grown throughout Europe, including Scandinavia, and in North America, North Africa, and northern India.

Celery seeds are tiny and practically weightless—there are close to half a million seeds in one pound. The curved ridged seeds, which are, in fact, split halves of the plant's fruits, are light to dark brown in color, with a penetrating aroma like that of stalk celery. They have a strong, warm, somewhat bitter flavor, although they are far less bitter than the seeds of their ancestor smallage. Cooking reduces the bitterness and enhances the sweetness of the seeds.

The seeds are usually used whole because they are so small, but crushing them will make them more aromatic. If they are ground, they should be used fairly quickly, as the flavor is fleeting and the bitterness will become more pronounced. The seeds are also ground for celery salt, which sometimes contains dried herbs such as parsley and/or dill (see sidebar, page 52).

The flavor of celery seeds complements tomatoes particularly well, and the spice is found in many tomato and vegetable juices (and, of course, in Bloody Marys). Celery seeds are also used commercially in ketchup, pickles, and numerous spice blends, particularly those for poultry and meats. They are often added to

(continued on next page)

salads or coleslaw or sprinkled over bread doughs before baking. In Scandinavia and parts of Russia, celery seeds are added to soups and sauces. They also season various Indian curries, especially tomato-based ones, and pickles and chutneys.

Caution: Celery seeds are used to make restorative infusions and tonics in India, but these should not be taken by pregnant women or anyone on blood pressure medicine or diuretics.

CELERY SALT Combine 3 parts salt and 2 parts ground celery seeds. Dried parsley and/or dill can be added for more flavor.

CEYLON CINNAMON

See Cinnamon.

CHAAT MASALA

Chaat (sometimes spelled *chat*) masala is a ubiquitous Indian spice blend, used to season everything from meat and vegetables to fresh fruit and salads. A typical mix includes amchur (mango powder), cumin, coriander, mint, ginger, chile pepper, ajowan, asafoetida, anardana (dried pomegranate seeds), cloves, salt, and—one of the defining ingredients—Indian black salt. It's a pungent, hot, sweet, salty mix made sour by the mango powder. Most popular Indian street foods, referred to as *chaat,* are seasoned with this blend.

CHAAT MASALA
amchur, cumin, coriander, mint, ginger, chile pepper, ajowan, asafoetida, anardana, cloves, salt, Indian black salt

CHAIMEN

See Armenian Spice Mix.

CHARMOULA

See Charmoula and Other Spice Pastes, page 183.

CHERVIL

BOTANICAL NAME: *Anthriscus cerefolium*
FORMS: fresh and dried leaves

A member of the parsley family, chervil is an annual native to eastern Europe. Sometimes called garden chervil to distinguish it from other varieties, the herb looks something like a cross between a fern and parsley, with delicate, wispy leaves. Its flavor is also delicate, with slight anise notes reminiscent of tarragon and undertones of parsley. The flavor of the dried leaves is muted, and they should be added in generous amounts to a dish toward the end of cooking; chervil, whether fresh or dried, does not stand up well to heat. Look for dark green leaves when buying dried chervil and avoid any hints of yellowing, which indicates age or improper storage.

Chervil is essential in French cuisine but little used in cooking elsewhere. It is particularly good in scrambled eggs and omelets—it is one of the ingredients in the herb blend fines herbes (see page 123), often used in egg dishes. It pairs well with fish and shellfish and is used in light cream sauces. It also complements spring vegetables such as peas, early carrots, and asparagus.

CHILES

BOTANIC NAMES: *Capsicum annum* (also spelled *annuum*), *C. frutescens*, *C.chinense*, *C. baccatum*, *C. pubescens*

FORMS: whole dried chiles, dried chile flakes, and ground dried chiles (pure chile powder)

All chiles are native to Latin America, particularly Mexico, and the West Indies, though they are now found around the world in tropical and temperate climate zones. Their history dates back to 7000 BC, and they were probably first cultivated in Latin America not long after that. But they were unknown beyond their native regions until Columbus took chiles back to Spain—and they then traveled throughout Europe and into Asia. Columbus thought chiles were related to *Piper nigrum,* the climbing vine that is the source of pepper, and because of that confusion, chiles are often referred to as peppers. The name chile comes from the Nahuatl word *chilli*—and the spelling still varies today, depending on the country, with *chili* being another form. Mexico remains a major producer, along with India, China, Thailand, Indonesia, and Japan.

Several hundred varieties of chiles have been identified, and the plants cross-cultivate and hybridize easily. *Capsicum annum* is the most common species, with *C. frutescens* second to that; some sources believe that these two originally came from the same species. (Other less-common species are listed above.) *C. annum* is an annual, and most chile plants are grown that way, but *C. frutescens* is more often cultivated as a perennial. Capsaicin is the compound that gives chiles their heat, and it is most concentrated in the ribs and seeds of the fruits. Generally, smaller chiles are the hottest ones and larger chiles less hot, but there are exceptions. The heat of a chile also varies depending on the climate, soil, and other

(continued on next page)

factors—and sometimes even chiles from the same harvest will vary in hotness.

Chiles are green when immature and will ripen to red, yellow, deep purple, orange, brown, or almost black, depending on the variety. They may be harvested when green or fully ripe. Dried chiles, whatever their locale, have traditionally been dried in the sun, either on mats or concrete slabs, or sometimes simply on flat rooftops. They are often left to cure out of the sun for several days before drying begins, and they are usually covered at night during the drying process (not unlike vanilla beans; see page 305). Another traditional way to dry chiles is to tie them into *ristras,* or garlands, or wreaths and hang them in the sun. While the traditional methods persist, today many chiles are commercially dried.

Chiles are used in cuisines around the world, from Mexico to the Mediterranean and Africa to Asia. They feature in salsas and hot sauces, spice pastes, and table condiments, and they season innumerable dishes. Although chiles are always associated with heat to one degree or another, they can also add complex flavor, and good cooks in any country choose their chiles carefully. Below are some of the most popular dried chiles, along with a number of more unusual varieties. (Note: As this is a book about spices and herbs, the focus is on dried chiles; other common chiles, such as jalapeños, that are best or only used fresh are not covered here.)

AJÍ AMARILLO (*C. baccatum*, sometimes identified as *C. chinense*; heat level: 7 to 8 on a scale of 10)

Native to the Andes, the amarillo chile is most widely used in Peru. Amarillos are usually more orange than yellow (despite the fact that *amarillo* means "yellow" in Spanish), and the dried chiles are orange. They are about 4 inches long and narrow, with a pointed tip. Despite their heat, they have a fruity flavor. The fresh chiles are often made into a paste that seasons a variety of dishes; dried amarillos are usually used in sauces. The dried chile is also sometimes known as *ají mirasol*.

(continued on next page)

THE SCOVILLE SCALE

In 1912, Wilbur Scoville, a chemist, devised a test to determine the perceived heat of chile peppers, which became known as the Scoville Organoleptic Test. Capsaicin is the compound that gives chiles their heat, and Scoville based his test on the amount of capsaicin per chile. Chiles were rated according to Scoville Heat Units, with bell peppers ranking 0, jalapeños ranging from 2,000 to 5,000, and superhot peppers like habaneros registering from 200,000 to 300,000 units. However, his test was based on taste and hence is a subjective one. A more modern test used by the scientific community employs a high-pressure liquid chromatograph (HPLC), which is far more reliable. Its results are given in ASTA (American Spice Trade Association) units, but Scoville's name is so ensconced in memory that these are often converted to Scoville units. Nevertheless, the heat of a particular chile can vary depending on growing conditions and a variety of other factors, and so results and rankings can vary greatly as well, with some sources, for example, giving a range of from 2,500 to 10,000 for jalapeño peppers. In this book, we use a simple scale of 1 to 10 to rate the heat of the chiles.

AJÍ PANCA (*C. baccatum*, sometimes identified as *C. chinense*; heat level: 1.5)

Panca chiles are widely grown along the Peruvian coast and are a staple of Peruvian cuisine. They are about 5 inches long and I to I½ inches wide. They ripen to a deep burgundy color, and the dried chiles are wrinkled and almost black. Panca chiles have only mild heat and a sweet, fruity, berry-like flavor. They are used in stews, fish dishes, and sauces.

ANCHO (*C. annum*; heat level: 3 to 5)

The ancho, the most popular dried chile in Mexico, is a dried poblano. It's a larger pepper, 4 to 5 inches long, and broad-

---

TOASTING AND SOAKING DRIED CHILES

Many recipes call for toasting dried chiles before using them, to bring out their flavor; the heat will often also soften the chiles slightly. Heat a large cast-iron or other heavy skillet over medium heat until hot, then add the chiles and toast, turning them once or twice, until fragrant, about 2 minutes. Remove from the heat.

Dried chiles are generally rehydrated before using. Put the chiles—toasted or not—in a deep bowl and add very hot water to cover. Let soak for 20 to 30 minutes, until softened. Often the chiles are then pureed in a blender (with or without other ingredients) with enough of the soaking water to give the chile paste or puree the desired consistency.

shouldered (*ancho* means "wide" in Spanish). It's usually deep red when dried but can be darker, and it is sometimes confused with the mulato chile (see page 69); it is also, confusingly, called a pasilla chile in parts of Mexico. Good-quality ancho chiles are still flexible, not completely dried. They have a fruity flavor and they tend to be on the milder end of the scale but can sometimes be surprisingly hot.

BIRD'S-EYE CHILE
This name can apply to any of a variety of small hot chile peppers, but it is most commonly applied to a type of Thai chile (see page 74).

BYADGI (*C. annum*; heat level: 6)
These chiles come from the town of Byadgi in the Indian state of Karnataka, in the southwestern part of the country. The dried chiles are around 2 inches long and bright to dark red. Like Kashmiri chiles, they are valued for the color they impart to the dish in which they are cooked, as well as for their fruity flavor and moderate heat, and, in fact, they are sometimes misidentified as Kashmiri chiles (and vice versa). However, they are noticeably thinner than the Kashmiri (they are sometimes referred to as *kaddi,* which means "stick-like"). Byadgi chiles are widely used in the cooking of South India.

CALABRIAN (*C. annum*; heat level: 3 to 4)
These chiles come from Calabria in southern Italy, a region known for its chile peppers. In fact, there are numerous capsicums grown there, but most of them are simply called Calabrian chiles. The dried chiles are deep red and usually 2 to 3 inches long. The red pepper flakes found in any pizzeria in Italy, called *peperoncini,* are usually

(continued on page 62)

CHILES
from left to right, top row: Calabrian, chilcosle, ancho, and
(clockwise on plate) bird's-eye and red and yellow chilhuacle;
middle row: Carolina reaper, aji panca, and whole and ground
cayenne; *bottom row:* aji amarillo, byadgi, and cascabel

from dried Calabrian chiles. American chefs cooking Italian food have recently become enamored of Calabrian chiles and are using them in many dishes. The dried chiles are also sold packed in oil.

CAROLINA REAPER (*C. chinense*; heat level: 10)

For the moment, at least, the Carolina Reaper holds the title for the world's hottest chile. It dethroned the Trinidad Scorpion (see page 75) in 2013, with a Scoville rating that averages 1,569,000 units but is sometimes as high as 2,200,000. The Carolina Reaper is a cross between a ghost chile (see page 65) and a red habanero. The dried chiles are about 1 inch long, wrinkly, and dark red. Proceed with caution!

CASCABEL (*C. annum*; heat level: 4)

The cascabel is a small round chile that gets its name from the way the seeds rattle inside the dried chiles—*cascabel* is the Spanish word for "rattle." It is also sometimes called *chile bola* (ball chile). The chiles are about 1½ inches in diameter, thick fleshed, and dark reddish brown. They have a slight smoky-sweet flavor and a nutty taste, which is accentuated when the chiles are toasted.

CAYENNE (*C. annum*; heat level: 8)

Most North Americans know cayenne chiles only in their powdered dried form, but the chiles—there are many different varieties—are grown in India, Asia, and Africa, as well as in Mexico, and they are especially popular in Indian and Asian cuisines. Cayenne chiles also grow in Louisiana and South Carolina, and they are widely used in Cajun and Creole cooking, and in hot sauces. The dried chiles are bright red, from 2 to 6 inches long, and narrow, with smooth skin—and very hot.

CHILCOSLE (*C. annum*; heat level: 5)

These chiles are a relative of the Mexican chilhuacle rojo (see below) and are also native to Oaxaca; their name is sometimes spelled *chilcostle*. They are about 5 inches long, fairly narrow, and often curved. They are thin fleshed and aromatic. Like chilhuacles, chilcosle chiles are most often used in moles and other cooked sauces.

CHILHUACLE (*C. annum*; heat level: 3 to 5, depending on the type)

Chilhuacle chiles come from southern Mexico—specifically the regions of Oaxaca and Chiapas—and are not often seen in the United States. They are thick-fleshed medium chiles, and there are three varieties: *amarillo* (yellow), *negro* (black), and *rojo* (red). Most are about 2 to 3 inches long, but some are more tapered than others. Amarillos have broad shoulders tapering to a point; they are reddish-yellow when fresh and dark red or almost brown when dried. They have a tart taste with some sweetness. Negros are squatter and look something like small bell peppers; they are a deep mahogany when fresh and a darker brown when dried. They have an intense flavor with notes of licorice. Rojos are red when fresh and a mahogany color when dried. They have a rich, fruity, sweet taste. All these chiles have complex levels of flavor, and they are most often used in the mole sauces that are the hallmark of Oaxacan cooking.

CHIPOTLE (*C. annum*; heat level: 5 to 6)

Chipotles are dried jalapeños, though other fresh chiles can be treated in the same way. The chiles are picked when ripe and smoke-dried. The larger chipotles also known as chiles mecos are brown and very wrinkled; they are 2½ to 3½ inches long and about 1 inch wide. They are hotter than the typical green jalapeño, since

(continued on next page)

they have ripened on the plant, and they have a fruity, smoky-sweet flavor. Mora and morita chiles are smoke-dried jalapeños, though moritas in fact may also be dried serrano chiles. Moras are slightly smaller than chiles mecos and moritas are just 1 to 2 inches long; some cooks think moritas have the most complex flavor. Chipotles are often sold canned *en adobo,* a sweetish, tangy tomato sauce.

COSTEÑO (C. annum; heat level: 4 to 7, depending on the type)

Costeños come primarily from the coastal areas of the Mexican states of Oaxaca and Guerrero (*costeño* means "coast"), and the chiles, which are usually dried, are little known outside their native regions. The dried red costeño, *costeño rojo,* also referred to as *chile bandeño,* is related to the guajillo chile. It is about 3 inches long, narrow, slightly curved, deep red, and quite hot, registering 6 to 7 on a scale of 10. The less-common yellow costeño, *costeño amarillo,* is bronze or amber in color when dried. It is usually less spicy than the red costeño, with a heat level of about 4, although it is sometimes hotter. It has a more complex flavor than the red costeño. It is used in some versions of *mole amarillo.*

DE ÁRBOL (C. annum; heat level: 7.5)

Also known as bird's beak chiles, these are one of the most popular dried chiles. The name *de árbol* means "from the tree," or "tree-like" in Spanish, and the bush that produces them can develop woody stems like a small tree. The bright red chiles, a close relative of cayenne peppers, are 2½ to 3 inches long, thin, and curved; the dried chiles range from bright to brick red. They are thin fleshed and very hot, with a smoky flavor. They are a good choice for chile oils or vinegars. The whole or ground dried chiles are used to season sauces, stews, and soups.

DUNDICUT (*C. annum;* heat level, 7 to 9)

These small chiles are indigenous to Pakistan, the major producer today. They are thin fleshed, round or tear shaped, and ½ to 1 inch in diameter. The dried chiles are scarlet and slightly wrinkled. Their heat level varies, but they can be very hot; along with heat, they add a fruity flavor to sauces, curries, and other dishes. Dundicuts are often compared to Scotch bonnet chiles, but they are not as hot.

GHOST CHILE (*C. chinense/frutescens* hybrid; heat level: 10)

Native to Bangladesh, the ghost chile was declared the world's hottest chile (from 850,000 to more than 1,000,000 Scoville units, depending on the harvest and the source of the ranking) in 2007, but there are more recent contenders for the title; see Trindidad Scorpion, page 75, and Carolina Reaper, page 62. In India, its names include *naga jolokia* and *bhut jolokia;* it is also referred to as Tezpur chile, for the region in northeastern India where it grows. The dried chiles are 1½ to 2 inches long, wrinkled, and red to dark reddish-brown, with thin skin. Obviously they must be used in moderation.

GUAJILLO (*C. annum;* heat level: 2 to 4)

The guajillo is the most common chile in Mexico. It is about 5 inches long and 1 inch or so across; the dried chile is deep red to mahogany in color, smooth, and shiny. The heat can vary from mild to fairly hot and the flavor is fruity but somewhat sharp. It is a thin-fleshed chile, and the skin can be tough, so sauces made with guajillos should generally be strained.

(continued on page 68)

CHILES
from left to right, top row: ghost, Kashmiri, de árbol, and costeño; *middle row:* dundicut, chipotle morita (*top*), chipotle meco (*bottom*), guindilla, and japonés; *bottom row:* ground and whole guajillo

CHILES (continued from page 65)

GUINDILLA (C. annum; heat level: 6 to 7)

These chiles are popular in Spain, especially in the Basque region. Long, curved, and thin, they are thin fleshed, with moderate heat and an underlying sweetness. Dried guindillas are used in Basque dishes identified as *al pil pil,* meaning "with chiles," such as *bacalao* (salt cod) or *gambas* (shrimp) *al pil pil.*

JAPONÉS (C. frustescens; heat level: 5 to 6)

Native to Mexico and used in Latin American and Caribbean cooking, these widely grown chiles are also cultivated in Japan and season many Japanese and Chinese dishes. The dried red chiles are about 2 inches long, narrow, and thick fleshed; some sources suggest substituting chiles de árbol for japonés chiles if they are unavailable, though de árbol are thinner fleshed and less meaty. Japonés chiles tend to have more heat than complexity of flavor. They can be used to make a spicy chile oil.

KASHMIRI (C. annum; heat level: 4 to 6)

From India's northernmost state, this chile is sometimes used as much for the color it imparts to any dish as for its fruity flavor and its heat, which is moderate. The thin-fleshed chiles are around 2 inches long, tapering to a pointed tip, and dark red and wrinkled when dried. They are often soaked in hot water to soften them and then ground to a paste before using, but they can also simply be dry-roasted until fragrant and added to a soup, stew, curry, or tomato sauce. Dried Kashmiri chiles are also available powdered, but be aware that the spice sold as "Kashmiri chile powder" is frequently a blend of different chiles, often not even from the region—check the label carefully.

MALAGUETA (*C. frutescens*; heat level: 7 to 8)

The malagueta is a hot chile from Brazil, and it is beloved there and in Portugal and Mozambique. It is sometimes called Brazilian hot pepper; it should not be confused with the Melegueta pepper from Africa's western coast, the source of grains of paradise (see page 137). The dried red peppers are fairly narrow and range from ¾ inch to 2 inches long; the smaller ones are sometimes called malaguetinha or piri piri peppers (piri piri is a name given to several different small dried chiles; see page 71). Malagueta peppers are the base of many Portuguese and Brazilian hot sauces (sometimes labeled "piri piri sauce"). They are used in stews and marinades in Brazil, Portugal, and Mozambique, and they are a favorite seasoning for chicken. (Also see the spice blend known as piri piri, page 236.)

MULATO (*C. annum*; heat level: 3 to 4)

The mulato is a close relative of the poblano and the dried chile is similar to the ancho (see page 58). Ripe mulatos have medium-thick chocolate-brown flesh and are around 5 inches long and 2 to 3 inches wide at their broad shoulders. The dried chiles are a very deep brown and wrinkled; their flavor is sweet, with notable smoky notes and a hint of chocolate. Mulatos are one of the chiles used in some classic mole sauces, notably the famous mole of Puebla.

NEW MEXICO (*C. annum*; heat level: 3 to 4)

There are several types of chiles called New Mexico chiles, many of which are cultivars developed at New Mexico State University. The most common dried New Mexico chile is a large red chile also called *chile colorado* (*colorado* means "red" in Spanish) or California chile. It is thin fleshed and dark red when dried; it is usually 6 to 7 inches long and about 1½ inches wide at its broadest point. Its

(continued on next page)

heat is on the milder side but noticeable, and its flavor is earthy and somewhat fruity. Dried New Mexico chiles are used in many sauces and often processed into chile flakes or powder.

PAPRIKA
See page 217.

PASILLA (*C. annum*; heat level: 3 to 5)
The pasilla chile is a dried chilaca pepper. It is dark brown to black, and it is also called *chile negro* (black chile). The word *pasilla* means "little raisin," referring to the chile's color and very wrinkled skin. Pasillas are thin-skinned, about 6 inches long by 1 inch wide, and slightly curved. The flavor is fruity, and the heat is medium to hot. Pasilla, ancho, and mulato chiles are known as the "holy trinity" for the classic mole sauces of Puebla.

PASILLA DE OAXACA (*C. annum*; heat level: 6 to 7)
These chiles are virtually unknown outside Oaxaca and parts of Puebla. They are sometimes called *chile mixe,* because they are grown in the Sierra Mixe. The chiles are picked when ripe and then smoked. The smoked dried chiles are deep red. They have a fruity, very smoky flavor, and are quite hot. They range in size from 1½ inches to 3½ or 4 inches long and are about 1 inch wide, tapering to a rounded or pointed tip. Larger ones are often stuffed, while the medium chiles are pickled. The small chiles are usually reserved for table (i.e., uncooked) salsas. These chiles are an important ingredient in Oaxaca's *mole negro.* Rarely seen outside their native region, they are worth seeking out.

PIQUÍN (C. annum; heat level: 6)

The name *chile piquín* (or *pequín*) is given to a variety of small chiles in Mexico; they are also called bird peppers. They are usually no more than ½ inch in length and are often smaller, but they are quite hot. The dried chiles are deep red to reddish-brown and thin fleshed; the flavor is smoky, with an undertone of citrus. Ground dried piquín chile is a common seasoning in Mexico, served as a condiment for pozole and other soups and stews and used as a garnish for salads and even some sweet drinks. *Elotes,* the popular street food of roasted corn that is slathered with mayonnaise and coated with grated cotija cheese, is typically finished with a sprinkling of ground piquín chile.

PIRI PIRI (C. frutescens; heat level: 8)

The chile known as piri piri, or peri peri, in Africa is native to South America, but it grows widely, both wild and cultivated, all over the African continent. *Piri* is the Swahili word for "pepper"; the chile is also sometimes known as the African Red Devil pepper or African bird's-eye pepper. The dried chiles are red, less than 2 inches long, narrow, and very hot. They are used to make hot sauces and in many traditional dishes.

PUYA (C. annum; heat level: 5 to 6)

The puya chile, also spelled *pulla,* is closely related to Mexico's guajillo chile (see page 65). It is 4 to 5 inches long and narrow, tapering to a sharp point (the word *puya* means "steel point" in Spanish). The dried chiles are deep red and spicy, with a fruity heat.

(continued on page 74)

CHILES
from left to right, top row: puya, tepin, mulato, piquin
flakes, whole piquin, and pasilla de Oaxaca; *middle row:*
piri piri, Thai (whole and powder), wiri wiri, and New
Mexico; *bottom row:* piri piri powder, Tien Tsin, pasilla,
Trinidad scorpion (*top*), and malagueta (*bottom*)

CHILES *(continued from page 71)*
TEPÍN (*C. annum;* heat level: 8)

Also called *chiltepín,* the tepín chile is a wild piquín chile found in Mexico and the American Southwest, although both *tepín* and *chiltepín* may be used to refer to any piquín chile in different parts of Mexico. The tepín is another bird pepper, very small but very hot. The chiles are about ¼ inch in diameter, thin fleshed, and red or reddish-yellow when dried. They are sometimes infused to make chile vinegar.

THAI (*C. frutescens, C. annum, C. chinense;* heat levels vary)

A number of different chiles belonging to several species grow in Thailand and while they range in size and color, most are hot, some searingly so. One of the most common is the small red chile often referred to as Thai bird's-eye chile, or simply bird chile. In terms of heat, it registers 8 to 9 on a scale of 10. It is widely used in other Southeast Asia cuisines as well. The dried chiles are added whole to stir-fries and other dishes and also used in sauces.

TIEN TSIN (*C. annum;* heat level: 9)

These chiles are native to Tientsin Province in China, and they are also referred to as Chinese hot chiles. One to two inches long and narrow, they resemble cayenne peppers. The dried chiles are bright red to scarlet and very hot. They are used in many Hunan and Szechuan dishes and are popular in other Asian cuisines as well. Because they are so hot, they are often removed from a stir-fry or other dish before serving. A spicy chile oil made with Tien Tsin peppers is used for stir-frying or as a table condiment.

TRINIDAD SCORPION, BUTCH T STRAIN

(*C. chinense;* heat level: 10)

The Trinidad Scorpion deposed the *naga jolokia,* or ghost chile (see page 65), as the hottest chile in the world in 2011, with a heat level of 1,463,700 Scoville units. However, its reign was brief—see Carolina Reaper, page 62. It is a cultivar native to Trinidad and Tobago. The dried chiles are ¾ to 1 inch long and dark red; the pointed bottom tip of the pepper is said to resemble the stinger of a scorpion, hence the name. The chiles have a pungent aroma and are searingly hot—use in moderation, perhaps to flavor a big batch of cooked salsa. Bottled hot (very hot) sauces are sometimes made with scorpion chiles.

WIRI WIRI (*C. chinense;* heat level: 6 to 7)

This hot chile from Central America has a variety of names, including bird cherry pepper, hot cherry pepper, and Guyana cherry pepper; the "cherry" part of the name obviously comes from its round shape and small size. It is particularly popular in Guyana, although it is used elsewhere in Central America and in the Caribbean. The dried chiles are about ½ inch in diameter, wrinkled, and red or reddish-yellow in color. The chiles can be reconstituted in warm water before being used, but they are fairly brittle and can simply be crumbled between your fingers or crushed and added to a simmering stew or sauce.

The **RED PEPPER FLAKES** [4] found on the grocery-store shelf—and in pizzerias—are most commonly crushed dried cayenne chiles, but other peppers, or a mix, may also be used. Beyond the familiar supermarket jar, however, there are a number of more exotic choices for adding heat and chile flavor to your dishes. Chile flakes from Turkey and Syria are increasingly appreciated in the West, and four types are described below, along with the Korean pepper flakes called *gochugaru*.

The **ALEPPO** [3] chile is named for the city of Aleppo in northern Syria, close to Turkey's southern border. The city is also called Halab, and the pepper is sometimes called Halaby pepper. The bright red coarsely ground pepper does not contain any seeds; it is often processed with salt and olive or sunflower oil, giving it a salty taste and a moist, clumping texture. It has mild to moderate heat and a very fruity flavor. Aleppo pepper has traditionally been used throughout the Middle East, especially in regions along the eastern Mediterranean, and in Turkey. Unfortunately, the worsening political situation in Syria means that Aleppo pepper production has suffered and the chile flakes are difficult to find.

The **MARAS** [5] chile comes from the town of the same name (also called Kahramanmaraş) in southeastern Turkey, which is quite close to Aleppo, and the pepper has a similar flavor profile. The bright red red pepper flakes, which may be coarse or relatively fine, have a fruity taste and medium heat. Maras (also spelled Marash) chiles have a high oil content, but oil and/or salt is often added during processing, and the chile flakes are moister and oilier than the typical dried red pepper flakes.

The **URFA** [1] chile also comes from southeastern Turkey, near the Syrian border. Named for the town of Urfa, or Şanlıurfa, it is sometimes called lost pepper. The chiles darken to almost a deep purple-black during the drying and curing process. Urfa chile flakes have a complex, somewhat fruity flavor, with undertones of smoke; they are often processed with salt, which complements their natural sweetness. Like the other chiles of the region, the peppers have a high oil content, and the pepper flakes are quite moist and can clump easily; as with those other chile flakes, olive oil is often added. The chile flakes are fruity and moderately hot, with a lingering heat. Most Urfa chiles are processed into chile flakes, so the whole chiles are rarely seen in the marketplace.

The Turkish **KIRMIZI** [2] chile is actually a blend of hot and milder dried chiles; *Kirmizi biber* translates simply as "red pepper." Oil and salt are added to the chile flakes during the curing process, and they are fruity, sweet, and moderately hot.

Korean red pepper flakes are called **GOCHUGARU** [6], or *kochukaru*. The coarse flakes are bright red and their heat can range from mild to moderate. The heat level may be indicated on the package: *maewoon* means "very hot," while those labeled *deolmaewoon* will be milder. They are an essential ingredient in kimchi, the spicy pickled vegetable condiment, most often made with cabbage, that is found on any Korean table. These chiles were traditionally dried under the sun, and the best versions are still sun-dried.

CHINESE ANISE

See Star Anise.

CHINESE BLACK CARDAMOM

See Cardamom.

CHINESE CHIVES

See Chives.

CHINESE FIVE-SPICE POWDER

Star anise is the dominant flavor in this well-known Chinese spice blend; the other spices are cassia cinnamon, cloves, Szechuan pepper, and fennel seeds. Some mixes also contain ginger, cardamom, licorice root, and/or dried orange peel. The powder may be fine or more coarsely ground, and the color ranges from reddish brown to tan. Five-spice powder is used throughout southern China and in Vietnam, as well as in some other Asian cuisines. It is good with fatty meats such as duck and pork. Many traditional Chinese "red-cooked" dishes are seasoned with five-spice powder. It is used both as a dry rub for roasted poultry and meat and in marinades. Fragrant and spicy, the powder should be used sparingly, to avoid an overpowering flavor of star anise.

CHINESE PARSLEY

See Cilantro.

CHIVES

BOTANICAL NAMES: *Allium schoenoprasum; A. tuberosum* (garlic chives)
OTHER NAMES: Chinese chives (garlic chives)
FORMS: fresh and dried or freeze-dried chopped leaves

Chives are an allium, a member of the family that also includes onion, garlic, and leeks. Regular chives, occasionally referred to as garden or onion chives, are native to central Europe; garlic chives, also called Chinese chives, are indigenous to Central Asia. Unlike other members of the allium clan, chives have almost no bulb, and only their long, thin leaves are eaten. Garden chives have long, bright green, hollow leaves, and their flowers, which are also edible, resemble pale purple or mauve pompoms; garlic chives, which can be slightly taller, have flattened pale-green stems and white flowers. Both have a more delicate flavor than other alliums, garden chives leaning toward onions in flavor, and garlic chives, not surprisingly, toward a more pronounced garlicky taste.

Fresh chives are used in many cuisines, but dried chives are almost as ubiquitous—particularly so since the advent of freeze-drying, which preserves their flavor and color much better than traditional methods. Most dried chives are garden chives, and freeze-dried chives will indicate that process on the label. Chives are very good in egg or cheese dishes, creamy white sauces, and salad dressings. They are one of the ingredients in the classic French herb blend fines herbes (see page 123), and they are often combined with other herbs. They should be added near the end of cooking in most cases, to make the most of their flavor. Garlic chives are used in a variety of classic Chinese and other Asian dishes.

CILANTRO

BOTANICAL NAME: *Coriandrum sativum*

OTHER NAMES: coriander, Chinese parsley

FORMS: fresh and dried leaves

Cilantro is an annual herbaceous plant indigenous to southern Europe and the Middle East. It is valued for both its fresh growth and its seeds, which, unusually, have a very different aroma and taste from the leaves; for more on the history and background of cilantro, which is sometimes referred to as fresh coriander, see Coriander, page 88.

Cilantro has bright green leaves that bear a certain resemblance to flat-leaf parsley, which accounts for one of its common names, Chinese parsley. But it is not related to parsley—it is a member of the carrot family—and its flavor is distinctive. It also seems to be divisive: although many people love cilantro, others think it tastes like soap. (According to some recent studies, an intense distaste for cilantro may actually be genetic.) Aficionados, however, find its unusual fresh, citrusy flavor addictive. Like most tender herbs, cilantro is best used fresh, added at the end of cooking to preserve its flavor. Dried cilantro has little fragrance, but high-quality dried leaves can impart something of the unique flavor of the fresh herb when added shortly before serving and allowed to "blossom" in the heat or steam radiating from the dish.

Cilantro is widely used in Latin American, Caribbean, and Asian cuisines; the stems and roots, as well as the leaves, are added to many dishes. Mexican fresh salsas and guacamole are flavored with cilantro, as are ceviches in Peru, Mexico, and other

(continued on next page)

countries. Cilantro is the Spanish word for coriander, and this may be why it is now used to describe the fresh leaf of the plant. It has a particular affinity for black beans and other beans. Its flavor is also good with hot chiles, and it is used in spicy stews and soups in Mexico and in curries, stir-fries, and other dishes in India and Southeast Asia. It is used as a garnish for lassis and the chopped salads called kachumbers, as well as made into chutneys in India and herb pastes in Thailand and other Southeast Asian countries, often in combination with garlic and/or chiles. Cilantro also pairs well with ginger, lemongrass, and mint, all signature flavors of Thai cuisine.

CINNAMON

BOTANICAL NAMES: *Cinnamomum verum, C. zeylanicum*

OTHER NAMES: Ceylon cinnamon

FORMS: quills and ground

True cinnamon comes from the bark of a tropical evergreen tree, a member of the laurel family, native to Sri Lanka. It has a long and venerable history, and it was known in the time of the pharaohs and in ancient Greece and Rome. It is mentioned in the Torah, and it was one of most sought-after commodities in the early days of the spice trade. Today, Sri Lanka is the main producer, and its cinnamon is believed to be the best. Cinnamon is also cultivated in other tropical regions, particularly the Seychelles. (See Cassia, page 48, for information on other members of the large Cinnamomum genus.)

The bark of the tree is harvested during the rainy season, when it is moist and easier to remove. "Cinnamon peelers" are highly skilled, and often several generations of the same family will be involved in the harvests, each generation learning proficiency from the one before it. Workers first cut the small branches, or shoots, from the trees and scrape off the coarser outer bark. Then the thin inner layers are cut and painstakingly rolled into scrolls, or "quills," and allowed to air-dry, protected from the sun. When the bark is processed, smaller pieces, called quillings, often break off, and these are inserted in the quills as the peelers form them. Quillings that break off as the cinnamon dries are used for ground cinnamon. Cinnamon bark is thinner and more brittle than cassia bark, and the fragrance is more delicate as well. The aroma is warm, sweet, and agreeably

(continued on page 85)

CASSIA AND CINNAMON
Indian and Indonesian cassia sticks, cinnamon sticks, and ground cinnamon

CINNAMON (*continued from page 83*)

woody, and the taste is equally warm. Unlike cassia, cinnamon bark can be ground at home in a spice grinder. The quills are paler than cassia quills, and the powder is pale tan rather than reddish-brown.

Cinnamon is one of the most common spices used for baking, from cookies to cakes and pies to sweet breads, and for other desserts. Whole quills are often added to the poaching liquid for pears and other fruits, and they are traditional in mulled wine. Cinnamon sugar is sprinkled over cookies or other baked goods. Cinnamon also has a wide variety of uses in savory dishes. Many Moroccan tagines are flavored with cinnamon, as is *bastilla* (there are many variants of this name), the savory phyllo-dough pastry stuffed with a filling of chicken, ground almonds, and rose water or orange flower water. Cinnamon flavors biryanis and other rice dishes, as well as meaty stews and curries, throughout the Middle East, India and Pakistan, and Malaysia; it is a favorite seasoning for lamb in many cuisines. Cinnamon is an ingredient in garam masala (see page 131), ras el hanout (see page 248), and many other spice blends.

MEDICINAL USES: Cinnamon has long been part of traditional medicine in Asia and India, and it was used for medicinal purposes in ancient Egypt as well. It is believed to help cure gastric upsets and is often prescribed for colds and other respiratory ills.

CLOVES

BOTANICAL NAME: *Eugenia caryophyllus*
FORMS: whole and ground

Cloves are the unopened flower buds of a tropical evergreen tree native to the Moluccas (aka the Spice Islands) in eastern Indonesia. They were an important part of the early spice trade (Columbus was looking for the Spice Islands when he landed in the West Indies). Their name comes from the French word *clou*, meaning "nail," because of their appearance, with a rounded head and tapered stem. Indonesia remains one of the largest producers, and the trees are now grown in Sri Lanka, Madagascar, Tanzania, and Grenada as well.

Cloves are harvested by hand, and the trees must be at least six years old before the first harvest, though they will then continue to bear fruit for fifty or so years longer. There are two yearly harvests, and the process requires a delicate touch. The buds are gathered when they have reached full size but have not yet opened, and they do not all reach the proper stage at the same time, so the pickers have to be discerning when choosing which clusters of buds to harvest. Then the buds are removed from the stems, again by hand, and dried in the sun for several days.

Dried cloves should be dark reddish-brown, though the bud end, which is surrounded by four "prongs," will be somewhat lighter. They are pungent and highly aromatic, warm and slightly peppery. The taste is strong, even medicinal, warming, and sweet; if chewed, cloves leave a lingering numbing sensation on the tongue. Good-quality cloves may release a small amount of oil if pierced with a fingernail. When purchasing whole cloves, avoid jars or packages with many noticeable stems, which have far less of the volatile oil than the buds. Ground cloves should be dark brown; a lighter color is an indication that the mix includes ground stems as well and is of a lesser quality.

Cloves are used in Middle Eastern, Indian, and North African cooking, in rich or spicy meat dishes, including Moroccan tagines, and in some curries, and they enhance many rice dishes. With their strong flavor, they should always be used sparingly. When the dish is served, the whole cloves may be removed or not, but they are generally not consumed. A clove-studded onion is often added to chicken stock as it simmers. Cloves are used in baking in Europe and North America, and in poached fruits and mulled wine. They combine well with many other spices, especially warming ones, and they are an ingredient in numerous spice blends, including garam masala, quatre épices, baharat, and berbere (see pages 131, 242, 24, and 31).

MEDICINAL USES: Cloves have been valued for medicinal purposes since ancient times, as a painkiller, among other uses (clove essential oil is still used to treat toothaches). They are also believed to alleviate intestinal distress, and they can be chewed as a breath freshener.

COCUM

See Kokum.

COLOMBO

OTHER NAMES: poudre de Colombo

Colombo is the name given to West Indian curry powders, specifically in Martinique and Guadaloupe; the blends are many and varied. Curry arrived in the Caribbean with immigrant workers from India in the mid-nineteenth century, and the name comes from the capital of Sri Lanka, Colombo. A basic mix consists of cumin, coriander, fenugreek, peppercorns, and mustard seeds; many blends include the decidedly non-Indian allspice, which is native to the Caribbean. Others may also include cardamom, ginger, cloves, turmeric, and/or ground dried bay leaves, and while some do contain dried chiles, others do not, as the dishes the blend is used for tend to include fresh chiles. In the West Indies, poudre de Colombo seasons curries made with goat, lamb, chicken, pork, or beef, as well as fish and vegetables. It is also used as a rub for grilled fish and meats.

CORIANDER

BOTANICAL NAME: *Coriandrum sativum*
FORMS: whole seeds and ground

A member of the carrot family, coriander is an annual plant native to the Mediterranean region, specifically southern Europe and the Middle East. It is an ancient spice, with a history dating back more than three thousand years; it is mentioned in the Bible and in Sanskrit texts (and in *The Arabian Nights*). It was one of the first spice plants grown in North America. Primary

(continued on page 90)

COLOMBO

clockwise from top: chiles, peppercorns, cloves, cumin, fenugreek, coriander, cardamom, ginger, bay leaves, turmeric, and mustard seeds

producers today include India, the Middle East, Central and South America, the United States, Canada, North Africa, and Russia.

Unlike those of most herbaceous plants, the seeds of the coriander plant have a very different aroma and taste from the fresh leaves. And while the leaves, often called cilantro (see page 81), are most popular in Asian and Latin American cooking, the seeds are widely used in many cuisines. There are two main types of coriander: Moroccan (*kazbarah*), which is more common, and Indian (*dhania*). The Moroccan seeds are pale tan to medium brown, spherical, and ribbed (looking something like miniature Chinese lanterns); the Indian are more oval in shape and range from a lighter tan to brown. The seeds have a warm, nutty fragrance and a sweet, somewhat pungent taste, with citrusy undertones of orange or lemon and faint notes of fresh sage; the Indian seeds are sweeter than the Moroccan. Both types have papery husks but are easy to grind, especially if they are first dry-roasted in a skillet. Coriander seeds are always toasted before grinding in India, but if they are to be used in baking and desserts, they should not be toasted. The seeds are best ground in a spice grinder, which will give a finer texture than a mortar and pestle. Ground coriander has a warm, mildly nutty fragrance and taste, again with notes of citrus.

Coriander seeds are harvested when mature, but the plants must be cut when the early-morning or late-afternoon dew is still upon them, or the seedpods will split. Then they are dried and threshed to remove the seeds.

Coriander is especially popular in Asian, Indian, African, and Mediterranean cuisines. It seasons curries, stews, and sauces, where it may also act as a thickening agent, and is added

(continued on page 92)

CILANTRO AND CORIANDER
fresh cilantro, dried cilantro, whole
Moroccan coriander seeds, ground
coriander, and whole Indian coriander seeds

CORIANDER *(continued from page 90)*

to chutneys. In India, it is used in drinks, and ground coriander is often dusted over raitas and lassis for garnish. Coriander is an essential ingredient in curry powder. It is considered an amalgamating spice, meaning it complements a wide range of other spices, and so it is used in many other spice blends as well, including ras el hanout (see page 248), and in dukkah (see page 108), the Egyptian spice and nut mix. In Europe and North America, coriander is more often used in baking and for pickling.

CUMIN

BOTANICAL NAME: *Cuminum cyminum*
OTHER NAMES: jeera, white cumin (see next page for black cumin)
FORMS: whole seeds and ground

Another member of the parsley family, cumin is an annual plant generally considered indigenous to the Middle East, although some sources say that it originated in the Nile Valley. Cumin is a major spice, and an old one—its culinary history dates back to 5000 BC. It was used by the ancient Egyptians in mummification and is mentioned in both the Old and New Testaments. It was also thought to encourage love and fidelity. Today, it grows throughout the Middle East and North Africa, with major producers including Iran, India, Turkey, and Morocco.

Cumin is harvested when the seeds have ripened, and the whole stalks are dried. Then they are threshed to remove the seeds and the seeds are rubbed, either mechanically or by hand, to remove most of the fine "tails."

Cumin seeds look like caraway seeds, and the two are

sometimes confused—the fact that the word *jeera* is used to refer to both spices in India adds to the confusion, though caraway is more properly called *shia jeera*. (For even more on mistaken identity, see black cumin, below.) The small seeds are slightly curved, ridged, and pale brown to greenish-gray, and they often still have some hair-like bristles, or tails, attached. They have a pungent, warm, earthy aroma, which becomes noticeably stronger when they are lightly crushed, and an equally pungent, lingering taste with a hint of bitterness. Ground cumin is reddish-brown and has a similarly strong aroma and slightly bitter but warm taste. Toasting the seeds before grinding will make the powder more pungent; ground cumin from toasted seeds is darker than powder from untoasted seeds and has a slightly smoky taste.

Cumin is an important seasoning in Indian, Middle Eastern, Asian, North African, and Mexican and other Latin American cuisines. It is used in couscous and merguez sausages in North Africa, in kebabs in many Middle Eastern countries, and in ground meat and vegetable dishes in Turkey. It is added to curries, stews, and other regional dishes throughout India, and it is used there in breads, pickles, and chutneys. It is an essential ingredient in spice mixes such as panch phoron and garam masala (see pages 214 and 131), and it is mixed with ground coriander to make the simple seasoning blend known as *dhana jeera*. Chili powder always includes cumin, as does charmoula, the Moroccan seasoning paste (see page 183).

Black cumin (*Bunium persicum*) is primarily grown in Kashmir, India, and it also grows in Iran and Pakistan. It is known as *kala jeera* in India and is sometimes called Kashmiri cumin. It is often confused with nigella, which is sometimes called black cumin but is an entirely different spice. Black cumin seeds are

(continued on next page)

darker, smaller, and finer than those of regular cumin, and their fragrance is less earthy and bitter. When the seeds are fried in oil, the taste becomes nutty. Black cumin is used mostly in northern Indian cuisines and Moghul-style dishes, such as biryani and korma, as well as in breads and some spice blends and pastes. It is also a seasoning in Pakistani and Bangladeshi cooking.

CURRY LEAVES

BOTANICAL NAME: *Murraya koenigii*
OTHER NAMES: meetha neem, kadhi patta
FORMS: fresh and dried

The curry tree is native to southern India and Sri Lanka, and its name gives rise to confusion on several fronts. A member of the citrus family, the tree is a small tropical evergreen, but there is also a curry plant from the same region, which is used more for ornamental purposes than for cooking. And while the leaves may be used in some curries and curry blends, they are by no means an essential ingredient in curry or curry powders.

Smaller than bay leaves, curry leaves are deep green. Their herbaceous aroma is reminiscent of curry powder, with an undertone of citrus, and their flavor can be slightly bitter, especially with longer cooking. When carefully dried, the leaves maintain their green color, although their fragrance will be muted; avoid dried leaves that have darkened or turned black. Fresh leaves are optimal.

Curry leaves are commonly used in southern India and in

Sri Lanka but are rarely found in the cooking of the north, although they do figure in some Gujarati dishes. They are an essential ingredient in many vegetarian dishes, including dals and lentil soups, and in curries. The leaves are often fried in oil at the beginning of cooking until very fragrant, but they can also be warmed separately in oil or ghee (clarified butter) that is then used to finish a dish. Unlike bay leaves, you can eat them whole or chopped, but younger leaves are best. Curry leaves are an ingredient in many pickles and in some chutneys. Left whole or ground with a mortar and pestle, they flavor marinades for seafood and lighter meats.

MEDICINAL USES: Curry leaves are important in Ayurvedic medicine and are prescribed for a wide variety of ills. They are believed to stimulate the appetite and to soothe indigestion.

CURRY POWDER

There are dozens, even hundreds, of curry powders found throughout India, most extensively in the southern regions, and in neighboring countries. Generic "curry powder" does not exist in Indian kitchens; instead, the spices and proportions of each blend are tailored to both the other ingredients in the dish it will season and the cook's personal taste. Madras curry powder may be the most familiar type to Western cooks looking beyond the generic jars in the supermarket spice section, but there are many others to explore.

(continued on page 97)

CURRY POWDER
1. Singapore
2. Madras
3. Vindaloo
4. Sri Lankan
5. Sri Lankan Dark
6. Malaysian

VINDALOO CURRY POWDER

This extremely hot curry powder usually contains coriander, cumin, turmeric, ginger, black pepper, cinnamon, nutmeg, and cloves, with a good proportion of dried chiles. Vindaloo was originally a spicy pork stew from Goa, on the southwestern coast of India, a legacy of the Portuguese explorers who landed there in the fifteenth century. They prepared a stew of pork marinated in vinegar and garlic called *carne de vinha d'alhos,* and as the dish acquired more of the local flavors, the name morphed into *vindaloo.* Vindaloo is now also made with beef, chicken, lamb, shrimp, or vegetables, although the curry powder is so hot it will overpower most vegetables.

SRI LANKAN CURRY POWDER

Sri Lankan curry blends do not typically contain dried chiles, so they are much milder than their Indian counterparts. For the most interesting version, however, the spices are roasted until very dark before grinding, which gives the mix an intense smoky aroma and flavor. These blends are much darker than other curry powders, and, in fact, they are sometimes known as black curry powder. Some powders are more lightly toasted, and the mix can also be made with untoasted spices, but the dark-roasting is what makes Sri Lankan curry powder unique. A typical blend includes coriander, cumin, cardamom, fennel, fenugreek, turmeric, and mustard seeds, along with dried pandan and/or curry leaves. This strong-tasting curry powder is especially good in beef curries, braises, and other heartier dishes.

MALAYSIAN CURRY POWDER

Curry came to Malaysia via Indian immigrants (many of whom were brought there by the British to work on spice plantations). A

(continued on next page)

typical Malaysian curry blend includes coriander, cumin, fennel seeds, cinnamon, turmeric, black pepper, cardamom, cloves, and dried chiles; the heat level, of course, can vary. Malaysian curry powder is used most often for chicken or vegetable curries, many of which include coconut milk. The Penang (or Panang) curries served in Thai restaurants in the West use a similar spice blend as their base; Penang is a state on Malaysia's northwest coast.

MADRAS CURRY POWDER

The heat levels of Madras curry powder can range from mildly spicy to very hot. A basic mix consists of coriander, cumin, dried chiles, turmeric, ginger, black pepper, cinnamon, nutmeg, cardamom, and cloves; some blends include mustard seeds and, occasionally, curry leaves. The whole spices are toasted and then ground, although many people in India today use fresh ginger separately instead of including it in the grounded blend. Madras curry powder is used in all sorts of meat, chicken, fish, and vegetable curries, as well as in other stews, soups, and rice or lentil dishes.

SINGAPORE CURRY POWDER

The cuisine of Singapore has been influenced by waves of Chinese, Indian, and Malaysian immigrants, and curry is very popular there. A typical Singapore curry powder is made with coriander, cumin, fennel seeds, fenugreek, turmeric, cloves, cardamom, and varying amounts of dried chiles; some also include rice powder. The mix can be used as a rub for grilled or roasted fish or meats, as well as in noodle dishes and all sorts of curries.

Also see Colombo (page 88).

MADRAS CURRY POWDER

cardamom, chiles, cumin, peppercorns, cinnamon, turmeric, ginger, cloves, coriander, and nutmeg

[D]

DAUN SALAM

See Salam Leaves.

DHANA JEERA POWDER

OTHER SPELLINGS: dhanajiru

Dhana jeera is simply a convenient blend of ground toasted coriander and cumin seeds. The classic blend uses two parts coriander to one part cumin. The spices are usually toasted ahead and combined, then ground as needed. Dhana jeera is widely used in the states of Gujarat and Maharashtra, on India's western coast.

DILL

BOTANICAL NAMES: *Anethum graveolen* (European); *A. sowa* (Indian)
FORMS: whole seeds and ground

Dill, a hardy annual that is native to southern Russia and the Mediterranean region, is a member of the same family as caraway, anise, and cumin. It was known to the ancient Babylonians, and a wide variety of medicinal benefits have long been ascribed to it. In the Middle Ages, dill was believed to have magical powers. Scandinavia,

(continued on page 105)

DILL
fresh dill, dill seeds, dill weed, and dill pollen

DILL (*continued from page 103*)

Poland, Russia, and Turkey are the major producers today, but dill is also grown in India and Japan, among other countries.

Dill seeds are oval, flattish, and tiny—ten thousand seeds weigh only about an ounce. The seeds, which are actually the halved fruits of the plant, are pale brown with lighter edges. Their faint aroma is reminiscent of their cousin caraway; when the seeds are crushed, they have a slight anise-like fragrance. The taste is pungent and slightly bitter. The dill that grows in India and Japan is a different variety from the European plant, and its seeds are longer and narrower. Dill seeds are usually sold whole, and they are used whole in most dishes. Once ground or crushed, their fragrance is fleeting. The seeds can be toasted before being used to bring out their flavor.

DILL SEED TEA Pour 1 cup boiling water over 1 to 2 teaspoons crushed dill seeds and steep for 15 minutes, then strain.

Dill features most prominently in the cuisines of Scandinavia, Russia, Germany, and Poland. The seeds are widely used in pickling, of course. Dill is also used in breads and goes well with potatoes and other starchy foods. It flavors soups and stews in Russia and Poland, and in India it seasons fish stews and meat and vegetable dishes. Dill complements fish and poultry, and it is an ingredient in many commercial spice blends intended for both of these. It is also one of the many spices in the Moroccan spice blend ras el hanout (see page 248).

MEDICINAL USES: Dill seeds can be chewed as a breath freshener. They are believed to aid digestion and have traditionally been used to treat a range of other ailments. In India, dill seed tea (see sidebar) is often prescribed to soothe stomachaches and colic.

DILL WEED

BOTANICAL NAME: *Anethum graveolen*

OTHER NAMES: dill

FORMS: fresh and dried leaves and pollen

Dill is an annual herb that is native to the Mediterranean and southern Russia; for more on its history and uses, see Dill, page 103. It is a relative of parsley, anise, and caraway. Its fronds look something like those of fennel, but the fragrance is reminiscent of parsley, and the flavor also echoes parsley, with undertones of anise. Dried dill has a grassy aroma and a similar though distinctive taste; in fact, some prefer the dried herb to the fresh. Look for dark green dried dill, and avoid any with signs of yellowing.

A sauce made with dill, whether creamy or vinaigrette-style, is a classic accompaniment to smoked salmon, and dill weed is also good with pickled herring, accentuating the flavor of the dill seeds often used in pickling. Dill weed also complements fresh seafood, particularly milder white-fleshed fish. Egg and cheese dishes are often flavored with dill weed, and it is a favorite seasoning for potato salad. Dill also pairs particularly well with cucumbers and green beans. It is a classic seasoning for borscht and certain other chilled soups.

Dill pollen is harvested from mature plants that have flowered and are then dried. It is simultaneously intensely flavorful and subtle; to preserve its delicate flavor, it is best stirred into a dish at the end of cooking or used as a finishing spice. Like fennel pollen (see page 119), another chef's favorite, dill pollen is expensive, but just a pinch or two will work wonders.

DRIED LIME

See Black Lime.

DUKKAH

OTHER SPELLINGS: dukka, duqqa

Dukkah is an Egyptian spice mix that also includes ground nuts and seeds. A typical blend contains hazelnuts, sesame seeds, coriander, cumin, black pepper, and sea salt. Hazelnuts or roasted chickpeas are the main ingredient in most mixes, but pistachios and other nuts are often included. Some versions contain dried mint and/or thyme. Dukkah is most often used as a flavorful condiment for flatbreads, which are first dipped in olive oil and then into the spice mix; or the dukkah can be mixed with oil and then served that way. It can also be used as a dry rub for chicken, fish, or steaks before panfrying or grilling, or applied more generously to make a crunchy coating. Dukkah is good sprinkled over salads, especially tomato salads; yogurt; and feta cheese that has been drizzled with oil. Until recently, specialty spice markets or Middle Eastern spice bazaars were the only source of dukkah—other than home kitchens—but Western chefs have increasingly been experimenting with the delicious blend (sometimes it even turns up on the shelves of stores like Trader Joe's).

EPAZOTE

EGYPTIAN
SPICE BLEND

EGYPTIAN SPICE BLEND

This popular blend can be made with a variety of spices, the choice and number depending on the spice merchant or cook, but a typical version might include allspice, black pepper, cardamom, cinnamon, cloves, coriander, cumin, ginger, and nutmeg, as well as dried rosebuds. These blends have a complex but delicate aroma and a rich flavor. They are used as dry rubs for grilled meats, poultry, and fish and are also added to soups and stews and to many lentil, grain, and bean dishes. A simpler spice blend, the Egyptian equivalent of the French quatre épices (see page 242), consists of allspice, cinnamon, cloves, and nutmeg.

EPAZOTE

BOTANICAL NAME: *Chenopodium ambrosiodes*
OTHER NAMES: pigweed, wormseed, Mexican tea, skunk weed
FORMS: fresh and dried leaves

Epazote is an annual native to Mexico, but it is also found throughout Central America, as well as in the South and other parts of the United States. It's a tall, bushy plant that is often treated as a weed, in part because it self-seeds readily and spreads easily. The leaves are narrow and serrated, with a distinctive aroma. The name *epazote* comes from the Nahuatl word *epatzotl*—*epatl* means "skunk" and *tzotl* means "dirty." No wonder it is often considered an acquired taste! Others compare its aroma to petroleum, creosote, or turpentine. But epazote is an essential herb in many Mexican black bean dishes. It is used in moles and long-simmered stews, in tortilla soup and other soups, and, in its fresh state, in quesadillas. When carefully dried, the herb retains its

(continued on next page)

EPAZOTE *(continued from previous page)*

characteristic scent and taste. When buying dried epazote leaves, avoid samples that contain a high proportion of the woody stems; if necessary, pick out the larger stems and discard them before crumbling the leaves into the dish you are preparing (or wrap the epazote in a square of cheesecloth and then remove it from your soup or stew after cooking). If it's not obvious at this point, epazote should be used sparingly.

MEDICINAL USES: Epazote can be brewed into a tea believed to relieve gassiness, but note the Caution below.

Caution: Epazote should not be consumed in large quantities; the concentrated oil from the plant has been reported to have negative health consequences; some have linked excessive use to kidney and liver damage, but any real connection remains unclear.

FENNEL

BOTANICAL NAME: *Foeniculum vulgare*
OTHER NAMES: common fennel, sweet fennel, saunf
FORMS: whole seeds and ground

Fennel is native to southern Europe, but wild fennel grows abundantly in many countries, and fennel has long been popular in China as well as in India, where it is known as *saunf*. Florence fennel (*F. dulce*) is the type eaten as a vegetable; common fennel, which provides the seeds, is a taller biennial or perennial plant that does not have the rounded bulb of Florence fennel. Today, major producers include Italy, France, Germany, Russia, the Middle East, and India, though fennel is also grown in many other regions of the northern hemisphere.

Fennel is harvested just before the seeds are fully mature. The stalks are cut and left to dry, usually in an area protected from the sun to preserve the color and flavor of the seeds, and then threshed to remove the seeds.

The small oval seeds are slightly curved, with prominent paler longitudinal ridges; the color ranges from bright green to greenish-yellow. When buying them, look for green seeds, which are of better quality. Some seeds may still have small stalks attached, but avoid jars or packages that contain a lot of bristle-like stalks. The aromatic seeds have a strong licorice fragrance and a

(continued on page 118)

FENNEL

116

FENNEL
dried, pollen, whole seeds, ground,
and toasted whole seeds

sweet anise flavor. Lucknow fennel, grown exclusively in Lucknow, India, is highly regarded. The seeds are smaller and thinner than common fennel seeds and the aroma and flavor are more delicate. Fennel seeds are usually used whole; toasting them, as is often done in India and Asia, makes them easier to grind.

Fennel seeds pair especially well with fish and seafood and are used to season both fish and cured fish throughout Europe. The seeds are one of the most popular spices in Italy, where they appear in finocchiona and many other cured sausages, as well as in traditional pork dishes. The seeds, whole or ground, are also used in breads, including a nigella-flavored bread in Iraq, and in many pickles, as well as in sauerkraut and pickled herring. Fennel seeds complement the flavor of tomatoes and season many tomato-based sauces in both Europe and India. They are also an ingredient in Indian curries and satay sauces. The seeds are considered an amalgamating spice, and they complement cloves, cinnamon, cumin, coriander, cardamom, fenugreek, and mustard seeds, as well as other warming spices, and ginger and chiles. They are an ingredient

FENNEL SEED TEA Pour
1 cup boiling water over 1½ teaspoons crushed fennel seeds and steep for 10 minutes, then strain.

in many spice blends, including Chinese five-spice powder, panch phoron, and garam masala (see pages 79, 214, and 131), and numerous curry powders and pickling spice mixes. The leaves are used in Syria and Lebanon to make an egg dish called *ijeh*.

Fennel seeds can be chewed as a breath freshener or a palate refresher. In India, Lucknow fennel seeds, toasted or raw, are often offered after dinner; Indian restaurants sometimes provide sugarcoated or sweetened fennel seeds. Fennel seeds are frequently an ingredient in *paan,* the betel leaf—wrapped breath freshener that is ubiquitous in India. The essential oil from fennel seeds is used in anisette, pastis, and other liqueurs.

MEDICINAL USES: Fennel is important in Ayurvedic and other traditional medicine. The seeds are considered a digestive and believed to relieve asthma and bronchial disorders. They are often infused into a soothing tea (see sidebar).

FENNEL POLLEN

Fennel pollen has become a favorite "secret ingredient" for contemporary chefs. The pollen is painstakingly collected from wild fennel plants once they flower and then dried. Most fennel pollen comes from Italy or California. The yellow powder has the flavor of fennel seeds but is far more intense and yet also more nuanced. It is excellent with fish and shellfish and very good with roast chicken or pork. It can be stirred into risotto or pasta or grain dishes, and it is used to season sausages and cured meats. It's expensive—understandably so, considering the harvesting method and the low yield from even a field of wild fennel—but you only need a pinch to transform a dish.

FENUGREEK

BOTANICAL NAME: *Trigonella foenum-graecum*
OTHER NAMES: methi, kasuri methi
FORMS: fresh and dried leaves

Fenugreek is an annual in the bean family. (For information about fenugreek seeds, see next page.) The dried leaves have a grassy,

(continued on next page)

nutty aroma. Look for intensely green dried leaves when buying fenugreek; a paler green is an indication of age, and the herb will have less flavor. (Be sure to store dried fenugreek in a dark place so it won't be bleached by light.) In India, the word for fenugreek is *methi*; the term *kasuri methi* is used specifically for the dried leaves. In Indian cooking, fenugreek is used both fresh, like spinach, and dried; it also figures in Pakistani, Iranian, and other Middle Eastern cuisines. It goes particularly well with potatoes and root vegetables. It is also mixed into doughs to make paratha in India and naan or other flatbreads in the Middle East. Fenugreek can be added to curries made with meat as they simmer or crumbled and sprinkled over meat-based curries or vegetable dishes for a final seasoning. It is often also added to lentil dishes throughout the Indian subcontinent.

FENUGREEK SEEDS

BOTANICAL NAME: *Trigonella foenum-graecum*
OTHER NAMES: bird's foot, cow's horn, goat's horn, methi
FORMS: whole seeds, crushed, and ground

The origins of fenugreek are not entirely clear, with various sources asserting that it is native to southern Europe, India, western Asia, and/or the eastern Mediterranean, but it is certain that it has been used for medicinal and culinary purposes since antiquity. A tall annual plant, it has been grown all around the Mediterranean region for thousands of years. Major sources today include Turkey, the Baltic region, South America, France, and Pakistan, as well as India.

Fenugreek gets many of its popular names from the shape of

the seedpods, which are 4 to 6 inches long, narrow, and beaked. Fenugreek is a member of the legume family, and the pods look like those of green beans (in Africa, the seeds are soaked and prepared like other legumes). Each pod contains ten to twenty small seeds. The seeds are yellowish-brown and roughly octagonal in shape, with a furrow running down one side, and they are so hard they might almost be mistaken for a handful of little pebbles. They have a pungent aroma, somewhat similar to that of celery seeds, and an astringent, bitter flavor. Actually, they smell like curry powder—or, to be more accurate, many curry powders smell like fenugreek. The seeds should be toasted before crushing or grinding, both to mellow their bitterness and to make it easier to grind them; be careful not to overtoast them, though, or they may become more bitter. Toasting also brings out some of the natural sugars in the seeds, giving them a slight aroma of maple syrup (fenugreek is used commercially to make artificial maple syrup). Use a spice grinder, not a mortar and pestle, to grind the hard seeds to the desired consistency. Ground fenugreek is orange-brown and very aromatic.

Fenugreek is used widely in Indian cooking, most commonly in curries, dals, and poultry and vegetable dishes. It is an important ingredient in various vegetarian preparations, as well as in breads and savory pastries, pickles, and chutneys. It also figures in certain Middle Eastern and Mediterranean cuisines, and in Egypt and Ethiopia, it is used to season flatbreads. Fenugreek is an essential ingredient in many curry and sambar powders (see page 272), in the Ethiopian spice blend berbere (see page 31), and in Bengal's panch phoron (see page 214).

MEDICINAL USES: Fenugreek is known as a digestive and has a host of traditional medical uses. Some believe it lowers blood sugar

(continued on next page)

and that it may be helpful in treating diabetes. It is also credited with increasing the flow of breast milk in nursing mothers, but it should never be taken medicinally by pregnant women (in the pharmaceutical industry, an ingredient in fenugreek seeds is used in the manufacture of oral contraceptives).

FILÉ POWDER

BOTANICAL NAME: *Sassafras officinalis*
OTHER NAMES: gumbo filé, gumbo filé powder

Filé powder is ground dried sassafras leaves. It is used to thicken and flavor classic Creole gumbo, the hearty soup/stew that is one of the signature dishes of Louisiana and popular in other parts of the South as well. The sassafras tree, which can grow to almost 100 feet tall, is native to the Gulf of Mexico. The Choctaw Indians of Louisiana were the first to use dried sassafras leaves as a thickener. Only the smaller leaves are used for filé powder; they are dried and then finely ground. Filé powder is added to gumbos at the end of cooking, off the heat—if boiled, it will become stringy. (Some cooks and chefs prefer to add a sprinkling of filé to each serving or to offer the powder at the table.) Filé powder can also be used to thicken other Creole or Cajun soups or stews. Store it in a tightly sealed container, as it can absorb moisture easily. Do not confuse sassafras powder, which is made from the bark and/or roots of the tree, with gumbo filé.

FINES HERBES

Fines herbes is a classic French dried herb blend consisting of chervil, chives, parsley, and tarragon; other herbs such as dill, marjoram, and/or lovage are sometimes included. (Various combinations of the same fresh herbs are also used in French cooking.) The mix goes well with egg dishes (there's an *omelette aux fines herbes* on every traditional bistro menu) and with poached chicken and fish. It is best added just before finishing a dish so as not to mute the flavors of these delicate herbs. Fines herbes can also be used to flavor creamy dressings or lighter sauces.

GALANGAL

BOTANICAL NAMES: *Alpinia galanga* (greater galangal), *A. officinarum* (lesser galangal)

OTHER NAMES: galangale; Laos root, galanga (greater); Chinese ginger, China root (lesser)

FORMS: sliced dried rhizomes and ground

Galangal is a tropical plant in the ginger family. There are several varieties; the two used in the kitchen are greater galangal and lesser galangal. Greater galangal is native to Indonesia, specifically Java, and lesser galangal to southern China. Today, galangal is cultivated in China and Southeast Asia.

Greater galangal can grow to as tall as 6 feet; the lesser generally reaches heights of no more than 3 feet. As with ginger and turmeric, it is the rhizomes, or underground roots, that are used in cooking. Although galangal was known in European kitchens in the Middle Ages, when it was called galangale, it is now rarely seen outside the countries where it is grown. It has been used for medicinal purposes since ancient times, especially in China (in parts of Asia, the powder was taken as snuff—a sure if somewhat unnerving way to clear one's sinuses).

After harvesting, the rhizomes are trimmed, with some of the skin removed to facilitate drying, and then dried, traditionally

(continued on next page)

GALANGAL

128

GALANGAL
fresh, dried, and ground

in the sun. Both types of galangal resemble ginger, but the skin is marked with horizontal rings or stripes. Fresh greater galangal usually has orange-red skin with darker rings; the interior is creamy and pale yellow. Lesser galangal has orange-red to brown skin, marked with pale brown rings, and the flesh is pale brown, sometimes with a pinkish tinge. Once dried, the rhizomes are polished to remove most of the remaining skin and then sliced or ground into a powder. The dried slices are brown around the edges and tan inside; the powder is brown or reddish-brown.

Greater galangal smells like ginger but has a more peppery, piney fragrance. The flavor is not as sharp as that of ginger and there are sometimes slight citrus notes. Lesser galangal is hotter than greater galangal. Ground galangal has a sharp, hot, slightly musky taste; it should be used sparingly. The sliced dried rhizomes keep well for up to three years. If stored airtight, the powder will retain much of its pungency for at least six months.

Galangal is an important flavoring in Thai cuisine, but it is also used throughout Southeast Asia and in China. Fresh galangal is an essential ingredient in many Thai curry pastes, and dried galangal is generally favored over ginger there in cooking. Galangal is also used in many Southeast Asian curries, stews, and soups, including pho, Vietnam's much-loved beef soup, and in fish and seafood dishes. It is an ingredient in many versions of sambal, the spicy Indonesian seasoning paste. It is also used in some liqueurs and bitters.

Kencur, or *kenchur,* another member of the family, is sometimes confused with lesser galangal. Its botanical name is *Kaempferia galanga,* and its origins are in Southeast Asia. It is not as hot as galangal, and it has noticeable notes of camphor or menthol. Kencur is most widely used in Indonesia.

MEDICINAL USES: Galangal is a traditional remedy for respiratory problems in Southeast Asia and China. It is also considered a digestive in many cultures.

GÂLAT DAGGA

See Tunisian Five-Spice Mix.

GARAM MASALA

Garam masala is one of the defining seasonings of northern India and Moghul-style cooking. *Masala* refers to a single spice or a blend of spices, and *garam* means "hot" or "warm," and the ingredients for the spice mix can vary from cook to cook. One of the simplest versions is made with either green or black cardamom, cinnamon, cloves, and black peppercorns. Others may also contain coriander, mace or nutmeg, cloves, and/or dried bay leaves, as well as both green and black cardamom. The mixture is sold as a blend of whole spices or as ground spices, and, either way, is incredibly aromatic and intensely flavorful. The spices are usually dry-roasted before grinding.

Garam masala is added to recipes at different points, depending on the form and the type of dish. The whole-spice blend is usually fried in oil or ghee before other ingredients are added to the pan, though the spices may simply be toasted before use. Whole-spice mixes are typically added to plain white basmati rice and rice dishes such as pilafs and biryanis. They are also used to

(continued on page 133)

GARAM MASALA
cloves, coriander, cardamom, nutmeg,
cinnamon, black peppercorns, mace, and cumin

season dals and other lentil preparations, as well as meat kebabs, chicken, and meat curries. The powdered mix can be used for any of the dishes mentioned here, and it can also be an ingredient in marinades for grilled or roasted fish. It is often used to season potatoes and vegetables, and many vegetarian dishes. Some cooks like to sprinkle a little ground garam masala over yogurt or salads.

GARLIC CHIVES

See Chives.

GARLIC (AND ONION) POWDER

Although garlic and onion powder, also called granulated garlic or onion, are not spices, many cooks turn to them as versatile seasonings. The powders are shelf-stable and easy ways to add flavor to a sauce, stew, or other dish. To make them, garlic or onion is simply dried and ground, although some brands contain an anti-caking agent. Either or both powders can be sprinkled over pizza, used as a rub for grilled foods, or mixed with softened butter for an aromatic spread. Garlic and onion powder are used in many seasoning blends, both homemade and commercial.

GINGER

BOTANICAL NAME: *Zingiber officinale*

OTHER NAMES: gingerroot

FORMS: fresh, dried rhizomes, dried slices, and ground

Although it is often referred to as gingerroot, ginger is actually an underground rhizome. It comes from a perennial tropical plant that is native to India or China, or perhaps both—its origins are unclear. However, it is clear that it is one of the oldest spices, and its use is widespread. Its botanical name comes from the Sanskrit word for ginger, *singabera,* which also means "shaped like a horn." China and India are the biggest producers today, but ginger is also grown in the West Indies, Africa, Hawaii, and northern Australia.

GINGER TEA Stir a generous ¼ teaspoon ground ginger and 1 teaspoon honey into 1 cup hot water.

Fresh ginger has pale tan skin and pale yellow flesh; the dried has brownish skin and a tan interior. The knobby branched rhizomes are often referred to as hands, and the smaller branches are sometimes called fingers. In the trade, the dried rhizomes are known as races. Ginger that will be dried is usually harvested eight to ten months after it is planted (ginger that will be used fresh or preserved is harvested several months earlier). It may or may not be peeled, bleached, or otherwise processed before it is dried, then cut into slices or ground.

Slices of dried ginger can be used to make a spicy tea or warming infusion. Some Indian chefs and cooks prefer to use the slices rather than commercial ground ginger, bruising and pounding the slices with a mallet or rolling pin and then grinding them, for a brighter flavor than that of powdered ginger that has been sit-

(continued on next page)

ting on the shelf. The flavor of ground ginger can vary depending on its source, but it is generally sharp, spicy, hot, mildly fruity, and aromatic; it is considered a warming spice. Although ginger is cultivated throughout India, the type from Cochin, which is widely exported, is usually considered the best. Jamaican ground ginger has a more delicate aroma and taste and is especially highly regarded. Lower-quality ground ginger may contain a lot of fiber and should be avoided.

In Europe and North America, ground ginger is most often used in baking and in desserts. Gingerbread and gingersnaps are the most obvious examples, but it is also used in spice cakes, scones and biscuits, puddings, and fruit dishes. On the savory side, many Indian and Asian curries are seasoned with ground and fresh ginger.

MEDICINAL USES: Ginger is considered a digestive and is said to help prevent motion sickness. Ginger tea (see sidebar, page 135) can be drunk to soothe a sore throat or provide a nice, warming lift, or it may be taken before traveling.

GOCHUGARU/KOCHUKARU

See Red Pepper Flakes, page 77.

GOMASIO

OTHER SPELLING: gomashio

A Japanese condiment or spice blend, gomasio is a coarsely ground mixture of black or unhulled white sesame seeds and sea salt (the word *goma* means "sesame seeds" and *shio* means "salt"). Some versions include dried seaweed. Gomasio is sprinkled over rice, vegetables, and salads and used as a seasoning in other dishes. It is used in macrobiotic diets as a healthier, lower-sodium alternative to plain salt.

GRAINS OF PARADISE

BOTANICAL NAME: *Aframomum melegueta*
OTHER NAMES: Melegueta pepper, Guinea pepper
FORMS: whole seeds

Grains of paradise come from a tall perennial plant that is native to the western coast of Africa, along the Gulf of Guinea. It is a member of the ginger family and related to cardamom. One of its alternate names, Melegueta pepper, comes from Melle, an ancient empire between Mauritania and Sudan, which the Portuguese colonists called Malaguet; the coastal region has also been called the Pepper Coast. Today, the plant grows primarily in Ghana and West Africa. The spice has been known since the thirteenth century, and it was used in Europe, often as a substitute for black pepper, for the next five centuries or so. Today, however, it is not often found outside its place of origin.

The fruits of the plant contain dozens of tiny seeds nestled in a bitter white pulp. The seeds are removed from the pulp and dried, traditionally in the sun. The seeds are hard, shiny, dark brown, and multifaceted, with a paler tip at one end; the interior is bright white. The whole seeds have a peppery fragrance with notes of cardamom; once cracked or ground, they are very aromatic, warm, pungent, and peppery, with a lingering numbness on the tongue.

(continued on next page)

Grains of paradise should be crushed or ground before using; toast them before grinding to bring out the flavor, if you like. Today, the spice is used primarily in the cooking of western Africa, but it can be substituted for black pepper in many dishes, imparting its distinctive flavor along with a peppery bite. Try the crushed or coarsely ground seeds as a rub for grilled steaks and other meats or add to stews and hearty soups (the Portuguese took grains of paradise to Brazil, and it appears in some recipes for feijoada, the national dish). Sprinkle some over homemade ricotta and serve it as a dip with flatbread. Grains of paradise are also good in mulled wine (they were traditionally added to warmed sack); they flavor some high-end gins, as well as craft beers and even home brews. They are one of the ingredients in the Tunisian spice blend qâlat daqqa (see page 242), which also includes black pepper as well as cloves, nutmeg, and cinnamon, and in some versions of the North African seasoning mix ras el hanout (see page 248).

GUINEA PEPPER

See Grains of Paradise.

GUM MASTIC

See Mastic.

GUMBO FILÉ

See Filé Powder.

HARISSA

See Charmoula and Other Spice Pastes, page 183.

HAWAIJ

OTHER SPELLINGS: hawayej, hawayij, hawayil

Hawaij is an aromatic, flavorful Yemenite spice mix, used throughout the Arabian Peninsula, notably in Israel, because of its Yemenite Jewish population. There are several different versions, some of which are available as whole-spice mixtures as well as the more commonly found ground forms. One that originated in Aden, a former British colony that is now part of Yemen, consists of ground cardamom, coriander, cumin, and black pepper, along with turmeric, which gives the mix its vibrant orange-brown color. Hawaij is used in many soups and stews and as a rub for grilled chicken, fish or seafood, and meats, especially lamb. Another popular blend includes saffron threads along with cardamom, turmeric, black pepper, and, sometimes, ground nigella and/or caraway seeds. It is good with lentils and other legumes. Other variations of hawaij are used for brewing tea or coffee.

HERBES DE PROVENCE

Herbes de Provence is a classic French blend like fines herbes (see page 123), but it consists of stronger herbs and is a more assertive seasoning. Fennel and/or celery seeds, dried lavender, marjoram, rosemary, basil, sage, summer savory, and thyme are the usual ingredients, but some blends are made with fewer herbs; although lavender is certainly traditional, some cooks find it overpowering and prefer to leave it out. Herbes de Provence makes a flavorful rub for meats, including steaks, or poultry that will be grilled; it is also good with roast chicken. It is added to some stews and is very good sprinkled over ripe tomatoes before they are roasted for tomatoes Provençal.

HING

See Asafoetida.

HOJA SANTA

BOTANICAL NAMES: *Piper auritum, P. sanctum*
OTHER NAMES: yerba santa, hierba santa, momo, acuyo, pepperleaf, pepper plant, root beer plant
FORMS: fresh and dried leaves

The hoja santa plant is native to Central America and goes by a variety of names throughout Latin America. It also grows wild in the American Southwest, and in southern United States it is sometimes called the root beer plant because of the scent of its leaves. The large, velvety, heart-shaped leaves have a strong anise flavor and a slightly peppery flavor—not surprising, since the plant is a

(continued on next page)

member of the pepper family. Hoja santa—the name means "holy leaf"—is an important herb in Mexican cooking, particularly in the southern part of the country, and is used in a variety of ways. The whole fresh leaves can serve as wrappers for tamales and other foods, imbuing them with the herb's distinctive flavor. They are also used in the green moles of Oaxaca, in pozole and other soups, and in seafood sauces. The flavor of the dried leaves is not as intense as that of the fresh, but they can be crumbled and used to flavor soups, sauces, and other dishes.

HYSSOP

BOTANICAL NAME: *Hyssopus officinalis*
FORMS: fresh and dried leaves

Hyssop is an ancient perennial herb that is native to the Mediterranean. It is a member of the mint family, and its flavor is slightly bitter, with sweeter minty notes. The plant looks something like tarragon, with long, narrow leaves, and both the stems and leaves are used (as are the flowers). Hyssop was originally valued for its medicinal uses more than as a culinary herb. It is good in soups and stews, such as cassoulet, and in other bean or legume dishes— crumble the leaves before adding them to bring out their fragrance and flavor. It can also be added, sparingly, to rubs for grilled lamb or pork. Hyssop is said to aid in the digestion of fatty foods (speaking of cassoulet), and it is used to make tisanes or herbal teas. It is also one of the many herbs in Chartreuse, the French liqueur that has been made only by an order of monks since the 1600s (the secret formula is said to list more than a hundred herbs and other plants).

INDONESIAN BAY LEAVES

See Salam Leaves.

INDONESIAN LIME

See Kaffir Lime Leaves.

JAMAICA PEPPER

See Allspice.

JAMAICAN JERK SEASONING

See Charmoula and Other Spice Pastes, page 183.

JAPANESE HORSERADISH

See Wasabi.

JEERA

See Caraway and Cumin.

JUNIPER

BOTANICAL NAME: *Juniperis communis*
OTHER NAMES: juniper berries
FORMS: dried berries

Juniper berries come from a small evergreen shrub that is native to southern Europe and the Mediterranean, as well as Norway, Russia, and North America. There are many different species, some of which grow wild all over Europe, but the major areas of cultivation today are Italy, eastern Europe, and Turkey. Juniper has been valued for medicinal purposes for centuries, and both magical and safekeeping properties have been attributed to it since biblical times.

(continued on next page)

Juniper berries are picked when they are ripe and have turned blue-black. They can take up to three years to mature on the bush, one reason that they are a relatively pricey spice; another is that they are usually harvested by hand, as machine-harvesting can crush the berries, and the plants have sharp, needle-like leaves, making picking the berries an arduous task. In addition, because of their long maturation time, both ripe and immature berries will be found on the same bush, so the pickers have to be careful to differentiate between them. Once dried, the berries may have a slightly dimpled appearance; they also often display remnants of a cloudy whitish bloom, but this is simply a harmless mold. The best dried berries are still slightly soft; avoid those that are rock-hard, as they will have little fragrance or flavor. The aroma of juniper is sharp, spicy, and piney, even turpentine-y, and the taste is equally sharp, slightly resinous, and bittersweet. More than anything, the smell and taste is that of gin—juniper berries are used to flavor gin, and the name gin is derived from the Dutch word for juniper, *genever*.

Juniper berries should always be crushed before using. They go particularly well with game, both game birds and meats such as venison or, in Scandinavia, reindeer, and are often used in marinades, rubs, or sauces for these. Their pungent flavor cuts the richness of fatty meats like duck and pork, and they are used in pâtés and terrines. In Germany and Alsace, the berries often flavor sauerkraut and pickles. They pair well with other spices, including rosemary, sage, thyme, and bay leaves, as well as with garlic and onions. In addition to flavoring gin, juniper berries are used in various liqueurs in Belgium, Holland, and Germany.

MEDICINAL USES: Juniper is used in folk medicine to treat intestinal problems, among other ills, and is considered an anti-inflammatory.

Caution: Juniper should be avoided by pregnant women and anyone with a kidney disorder (it has sometimes been prescribed as a diuretic).

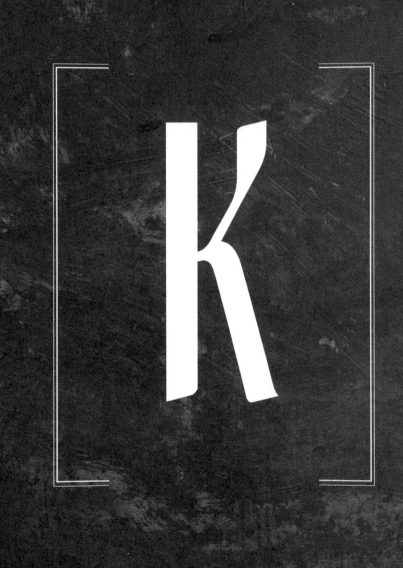

KAFFIR LIME LEAVES

BOTANICAL NAME: *Citrus hystrix*
OTHER NAMES: wild lime, Indonesian lime, makrut
FORMS: fresh and whole and ground dried leaves

The kaffir lime tree is native to Southeast Asia, as is all citrus, but, unlike with other citrus fruits, traditionally only the zest—not the pulp and juice—was used, along with the leaves, which are used fresh or dried. The double-lobed leaves are unusual looking, composed of two oval leaves growing end to end. They are dark green, shiny, and very aromatic. Their fragrance is that of a blend of citrus fruits, a strong lime scent with lemony undertones, and it is also reminiscent of lemongrass or lemon verbena; the flavor is clean, sharp, and citrusy.

The dried leaves are not as aromatic as the fresh, but if they have been properly treated, they will add their characteristic citrus tang to a variety of dishes. Dried kaffir lime leaves are sold both whole and ground.

Kaffir lime leaves are widely used in Indonesia and Thailand, as well as in Vietnam and some other regions of Southeast Asia. Many versions of pho, the classic Vietnamese beef broth, include kaffir lime, and it flavors other soups, stews, stir-fries, and

(continued on page 160)

curries. If the leaves are added whole to the dish, they are often removed before serving.

Note: Although the tree is commonly known as kaffir lime in the West, *kaffir* is a derogatory term in South Africa that many prefer to avoid, calling it wild lime or Indonesian lime instead. *Makrut* is the Thai name, and the leaves are sometimes identified that way.

KALONGI

See Nigella.

KAPOK BUDS

See Marathi Moggu.

KENCUR

See Galangal.

KASHMIRI MASALA

Kashmiri masala is a spice blend used to season many dishes in India's northernmost state, including elaborate Moghul-style preparations. A more complex blend may include coriander, cumin, garlic, turmeric, black pepper, dried chiles (preferably Kashmiri chiles), cinnamon, nutmeg and/or mace, fennel, and cloves, but there are many simpler versions as well. Kashmiri masala is the essential seasoning for *rogan josh,* the region's famous lamb curry.

KHMELI-SUNELI

Khmeli-suneli is a classic spice and herb blend from Georgia that is popular throughout the Caucasus regions. The name translates literally as "dried spice," and the mix, a coarse powder, is found in many incarnations. Fenugreek (both seeds and dried leaves), savory (winter or summer), black pepper, hyssop, and coriander are considered basic ingredients, but most blends contain many more, such as marjoram, mint, bay leaves, parsley, and/or dill, and dried marigolds are often included. The aroma is complex, and the flavor is warm and grassy. Khmeli-suneli is the defining seasoning for *karcho,* a hearty soup made with beef, lamb, or chicken, and it is essential in *satsivi,* a walnut sauce that is part of many dishes. It also seasons *chahohbili,* a traditional chicken stew, and other stews, and it is very good with dried beans.

KIRMIZI CHILE

See Red Pepper Flakes, page 77.

KOKUM

BOTANICAL NAME: *Garcinia indica*
OTHER SPELLINGS: kokam, cocum
FORMS: semidried and dried

Kokum is the fruit of a tropical evergreen tree native to India's western coast; in fact, it grows only in India and is virtually unknown elsewhere. It is related to the mangosteen, and it bears purple fruits that look like small plums or passion fruits.

(continued on page 163)

KOKUM
semidried and dried

The fruits are picked when they are ripe. Then they are halved, the pulp is removed, and the rinds are dried in the sun; often they are rubbed with salt to hasten the drying process. The fruit darkens as it dries, turning dark purple to black. Black kokum is the form most often found; it is also called wet kokum, and the rinds are still pliable and moist. White kokum is dried longer and it is also known simply as dried kokum; sometimes these fruits have been cut into slices rather than halved, and they will still contain their hard whitish seeds, which should be removed before use.

Kokum is primarily used as a souring agent, though it also adds a pinkish-purple color to any dish seasoned with it. It has a tart, slightly sweet, astringent flavor. Black kokum that has been salted during the drying process can be quite salty and should be rinsed before using. White kokum is usually soaked before being used to soften it, making it easier to remove the seeds. Kokum is used in the cuisines of Gujarat, Goa, and other coastal and southern Indian states. There it is added to curries, especially fish curries, and to legume and vegetable dishes. Its flavor pairs well with coconut, and kokum-flavored coconut milk is sold as a refreshing drink in India; kokum sherbet is also popular in the hot southern regions.

LA KAMA

La kama is a Moroccan spice blend that is a far simpler combination than the more well-known ras el hanout (see page 248). A typical version consists of black pepper, ginger, turmeric, cinnamon, and nutmeg, but, as with many North African spice blends, the ingredients can vary from cook to cook (or spice merchant to spice merchant). Some blends also contain mace; others omit the cinnamon and add cumin. La kama has a warm, very aromatic, peppery fragrance and a sweet-hot taste. It is used in tagines made with lamb, chicken, or fish and in many stews and soups, notably *harira*, traditionally served to break the Ramadan fast. La kama can also be used as a rub for grilled lamb, chicken, or fish.

LAVENDER

BOTANICAL NAMES: *Lavandula angustifolia, L. officinalis* (English); *L. dentata* (French)
FORMS: fresh and dried flowers and buds

Lavender, a member of the mint family, is one of most aromatic of all herbs. There are many different species, but all are native to the Mediterranean; English and French lavender are the types

(continued on page 170)

LAVENDER
fresh and dried

preferred for cooking. Lavender is mentioned in the Bible, and it was used by the ancient Greeks and Romans. Today, France is the major producer, and beautiful fields of lavender in bloom, with its fragrant purple flowers, are a part of the landscape of southern France.

The flowers and buds of the plant, not the leaves, are used. Their intense fragrance is sweet and floral, and their flavor is also floral, with camphor-like, piney undertones. Dried lavender is almost as potent as fresh. Lavender is well-known for its use in soaps, potpourri, and the like, but it does have a place in the kitchen. It helps cut the richness of fatty meats and game, and it can be used, on its own or with other dried herbs, as a rub for grilled or roasted meats. It is one of the ingredients in the classic French blend herbes de Provence (see page 145). Lavender is also good in desserts and is often infused in cream or milk to be used as the base of a custard or ice cream. Lavender shortbread cookies and scones are delicious.

LEMON VERBENA

BOTANICAL NAME: *Aloysia triphylla* (formerly *Lippia citriodora*)
FORMS: fresh and dried leaves

Lemon verbena is a shrub that is native to South America; it was brought to Europe by Spanish explorers and is now grown widely in France, as well as in England. It is related to verbena, *Verbena officinalis* (also called vervain or, in France, *verveine*), but the two should not be confused. Lemon verbena can grow to as tall as 15 feet. Its pale green leaves are about ½ inch long, narrow, pointed, and wonderfully aromatic. They have an intense lemon fragrance and taste, without the citrus acidity. The dried leaves retain their scent and flavor well.

Lemon verbena is used in potpourri and similar fragrant herb mixtures; the dried leaves are often made into a tisane, or restorative tea. In cooking, it can be added to the poaching liquid for fish or chicken, and because of its strong lemon flavor, some sources suggest it as a substitute for lemongrass in Asian dishes when that is unavailable. But lemon verbena is more often used in desserts. It can be infused into the liquid for custards or ice cream or made into a fragrant citrus curd. It can also be used in the syrup for poached fruit or to flavor a creamy rice pudding. It adds a bright note to summer drinks and other beverages.

LEMONGRASS
fresh, ground dried, finely sliced dried,
and sliced dried

LEMONGRASS

BOTANICAL NAME: *Cymbopogon citratus*
FORMS: fresh and sliced or ground dried stalks

Lemongrass is a tall tropical grass native to Asia; it is now also grown in central Africa, South America, the West Indies, India, and in the United States, Florida. The fibrous stalks are very fragrant—lemongrass contains citral, a compound that is also found in lemon peel. The lower parts of the stalks have the most flavor. Dried lemongrass is sold sliced into rings or ground into a powder; unfortunately, it loses much of its fresh, clean, lemony aroma and taste when dried.

Lemongrass is widely used in Thai, Vietnamese, Malaysian, Indonesian, and other Asian cuisines. It is sometimes found in markets under its Indonesian name, *sereh*. Dried lemongrass can be substituted for fresh in some soups and stews; if using the powder, add it sparingly. Dried lemongrass can be used to infuse boiling water to make a refreshing herbal tea.

LICORICE ROOT

BOTANICAL NAME: *Glycyrrhiza glabra*
OTHER NAMES: sweetroot, sweetwood
FORMS: sliced dried root, sticks, and powder

Licorice is an herbaceous annual in the bean family. Native to the Middle East, southwestern Asia, and southern Europe, it has been valued for medicinal and culinary uses since ancient times. The Greek name for licorice means "sweet root." There are other varieties of *Glycyrrhiza*, but *G. glabra* is the type preferred for use

(continued on next page)

in the kitchen. Today, licorice is grown throughout the Middle East and Asia, in southern Europe, and in the western United States.

Although the plant develops small pods containing five seeds each, only the roots are used. They are harvested once the plants are three or four years old, cleaned, trimmed, and dried. The straight lengths of the roots are sold as licorice sticks (not to be confused with dark black licorice sticks that are actually dried concentrated licorice extract). The remaining roots are sliced, chopped, or ground into a powder or used to make licorice extract. The dried roots have brown skin and a pale tan interior; powdered licorice is pale brown to grayish-green. The roots smell like tobacco—licorice is actually used as a flavoring agent in cigarettes—but immediately release a sweet taste when bitten into; the flavor is similar to that of fennel or anise. The powder is very pungent. (It attracts moisture readily, so it should be stored in an airtight container.)

Licorice root has been used since Greek and Roman times, prescribed to soothe sore throats and coughs, chewed on for its sweet taste, and brewed into a refreshing drink. Today, it is important in the confectionery industry, but its medicinal benefits have overshadowed its culinary use in most countries, including India as well as China, where it was well-known to herbalists centuries ago. However, licorice is an ingredient in some Asian master stocks, and it can be added to the poaching liquid for pears and other fruit. In Spain's Basque region, sharpened skewers of licorice root are sometimes used for grilling meat, imbuing it with their flavor as it cooks. The roots can also be steeped in milk or cream to make a base for ice cream or custard.

MEDICINAL USES: Licorice root is prescribed in Ayurvedic medicine for a variety of ailments, from intestinal distress to liver problems, and to clean teeth, and it is believed to be an anti-inflammatory. It should be avoided by anyone with high blood pressure, heart disease, or kidney problems.

LOOMI

See Black Lime.

MACE

BOTANICAL NAME: *Myristica fragrans*
FORMS: whole dried blades and ground

The nutmeg tree, native to the Spice Islands, is the source of a second lesser-known spice as well, and that is mace. (See Nutmeg, page 200, for more about the history and provenance of the tree, as well as more details on the harvesting process.) The seed, or kernel, nestled inside the fruit of the tree is enveloped in a lacy covering, or aril, of what are called mace blades, which are bright red when the fruit is first split open. This covering is carefully removed, pressed flat, and dried in the sun in a matter of hours. Then the mace is either left whole or ground. The fully dried blades are an orange-red or orange-yellow; ground mace is orangey-brown in color.

Like nutmeg, mace has a warm fragrance and a similarly warming taste, but it is somewhat lighter, fresher, and more aromatic; it has a slightly bitter undertone. In Western markets, ground mace is by far the more common form of the spice, and that is the way it is used in most cuisines. It is difficult to grind the blades at home; if you want to attempt that, use a spice grinder rather than a mortar and pestle.

(continued on page 185)

MACE

188

CHARMOULA AND OTHER SPICE PASTES

There are dozens of spice blends made with dried spices, from garam masala to quatre épices, but some classic seasoning blends from around the world are made with fresh ingredients as well and pounded or processed to a paste. Here are some that you might like to try.

CHARMOULA (also spelled chermoula) is a hallmark of Moroccan cooking, used as both a marinade, usually for fish or shellfish, and a condiment or table sauce. A basic version might include cumin and coriander seeds, paprika, salt, garlic, lemon juice, and oil (shown at left [1] is a blend of ground charmoula spices). Some also include cayenne or chiles for more heat, and/or ginger, and often fresh herbs, such as cilantro and parsley, are added. There is a charmoula made with fresh mint, and another one with tomatoes. Usually the ingredients are pounded to a paste using a mortar and pestle (or, today, in a blender), but occasionally the consistency is more like that of a chunky salsa. There are also cooked versions, simmered into sauce. Traditionally, charmoula was used to preserve certain foods as well as to season them, and those versions usually included vinegar. All are vibrant and delicious.

HARISSA [2, ground dried chiles and spices; 3, paste] is a fiery-hot Tunisian spice paste that is also widely used in Moroccan and Algerian cooking; precise blends may vary from cook to cook or country to country. It most often accompanies tagines and couscous, but it is also served as a table condiment—to be used sparingly! Dried hot chiles and garlic are the base ingredients, and the other seasonings usually include cumin, coriander, and caraway seeds; many versions contain mint. The chiles are soaked and drained, then pounded or blended with the other ingredients, along with olive oil. Regional variations abound; some versions include paprika, others add cassia/cinnamon.

JAMAICAN JERK SEASONING [4] may simply be a combination of ground and crushed spices used as a dry rub, but a more common version is a wet marinade made with scallions and/or onions, fresh chiles, and often garlic. In all cases, allspice is an essential seasoning; other spices may include cinnamon, ginger, nutmeg, and/or cloves, along with salt. Once the ingredients are pounded or blended to a paste, water or even rum may be added for a looser consistency. The meat of choice, usually chicken or pork, is rubbed with the paste and allowed to marinate for an hour or more before it is grilled. Some cooks add tamarind, others include brown or white sugar; the variations are many and personal.

ZHUG (or zhoug) [5] is a spicy Yemenite paste that is used both as a marinade or rub for grilled fish or meat and as a table condiment for various dishes. It is also served with flatbreads. The heat may be on the milder side or intense, depending on the cook and the dish. A basic mix includes both hot chiles and milder peppers, coriander and cardamom seeds, garlic, fresh cilantro, and, sometimes, lemon juice. The fresh ingredients are chopped as necessary and then all are blended or pounded to a paste. Zhug is sometimes combined with tomatoes to make a sauce.

Mace is used to flavor both sweet and savory dishes. The whole blades can be used to infuse cream or milk for a custard and then strained out; they can also flavor stocks or soups. Whole blades are also added to braises and other slow-cooked meat dishes. Ground mace can be used as the seasoning for a béchamel sauce, rather than the traditional nutmeg, and it is good in other creamy sauces. It is an ingredient in many cakes, cookies, and other baked goods, as well as in fillings for pumpkin or squash pies. It pairs well with seafood and poultry, and in the Middle East, it often seasons lamb or mutton dishes.

MAHLAB

BOTANICAL NAME: *Prunus mahaleb*
OTHER NAMES: mahleb, mahlebi, mahlepi, St. Lucie's cherry
FORMS: whole kernels and ground

This unusual spice is actually the pits of the fruits of a tall wild cherry tree that is native to southern Europe and Turkey. The cherries are small, sour, and so tart that they are usually harvested only for their pits. Today, the trees grow mainly in Iran, Turkey, and Syria and across the Mediterranean region.

The pits, which are about ¼ inch long, oval, and slightly tear shaped, are blanched and dried, then left whole or ground. Whole pits, which are pale brown on the outside and white inside, are quite aromatic, with a sweet, flowery fragrance that evokes cherries and almonds. They are soft and chewy and taste a bit like cherries, with a nutty bitter-almond undertone; the aftertaste, though, can be quite bitter. Ground mahlab may be slightly coarse or as fine as flour, and it ranges from creamy white

(continued on next page)

to pale tan in color. The powder loses its fragrance and flavor quite quickly, so it's best to buy mahlab whole and grind it yourself before using.

Mahlab is used in Greek, Turkish, and Middle Eastern baked goods, and sometimes in ice creams (especially chocolate). In Greece and Turkey, it is an ingredient in breads, particularly festive Easter breads, and in cakes and cookies. Because it is so aromatic, a pinch or so of the powder is all that is needed in most recipes. In Egypt, mahlab flavors a sweet paste made with sesame seeds, nuts, and honey, and in many countries, it flavors pastries and sweets eaten to celebrate the end of Ramadan. Mahlab is also used in some savory preparations, including rice dishes.

MAKRUT

See Kaffir Lime Leaves.

MANGO POWDER

See Amchur.

MARAS CHILE

See Red Pepper Flakes, page 77.

MARATHI MOGGU

BOTANICAL NAME: *Bombax ceiba*
OTHER NAMES: kapok buds, Andhra mogga, karer, shalmali, semul
FORMS: dried buds

Marathi moggu are the dried unopened buds of a tree popularly known as the red silk cotton tree or cotton tree, or, sometimes, the kapok tree. The tree is native to South India, specifically the state of Karnataka, and the buds are used in the cooking of Karnataka and Andhra Pradesh but rarely seen elsewhere.

The dried buds look somewhat like fat nails or, perhaps, tiny plump sabers with long handles. They are dark brown and hard. Marathi moggu buds are sometimes described as a type of caper, but they are not at all related. The flavor is something like a combination of mustard and black pepper.

Marathi moggu buds are used in traditional southern Indian recipes, including biryanis and other rice dishes. The buds may be fried in oil before other ingredients are added, but they are more often first toasted and ground and then combined with other spices. They are an ingredient in some curry and masala mixes.

MARJORAM

BOTANICAL NAME: *Origanum majorana*
OTHER NAMES: sweet marjoram, knotted marjoram
FORMS: fresh and dried leaves

Like its close cousin oregano, marjoram is an ancient herb native to the Mediterranean. A member of the mint family, it is a perennial that bears tiny white flowers in the summer. The deep

(continued on next page)

green leaves are aromatic and somewhat reminiscent of thyme. Sweet marjoram is the most common variety, but knotted marjoram flourishes in many herb gardens; the type called pot marjoram has a less agreeable taste and is better passed over for either of the other two. The flavor of marjoram is somewhat more delicate than that of oregano, but as is true of oregano, its flavor intensifies when dried. Some cooks prefer the more concentrated taste of dried marjoram to fresh.

Marjoram can be used in many of the same ways as oregano; see page 205. It is especially popular in Italy and Greece, where it seasons tomato-based sauces and other dishes. It is an ingredient in various Italian herb blends and is sometimes added to a bouquet garni (see page 36). Marjoram is good with fatty meats like pork and with duck and goose, as well as in poultry stuffings. It pairs well with other Mediterranean herbs such as rosemary, sage, savory, thyme, and, of course, oregano.

MASTIC

BOTANICAL NAME: *Pistacia lentiscus*
OTHER NAMES: gum mastic, mastiha, mastika, mastekah, miskeh
FORMS: tears (drops)

Mastic is the hardened resin of various species of the gum mastic tree, a hardy evergreen native to the Mediterranean and the Middle East. Today, however, most mastic comes from the Greek island of Chios, where production is still largely a family affair but is strictly controlled by the Gum Mastic Growers' Association (mastic from the Chios growers has been trademarked under the Greek name *mastiha*).

To tap the resin, cuts are made in the bark of the trees over a two- or three-month period from July into August and sometimes September, and the resin that emerges gradually coagulates (similarly to asafoetida; see page 19). Then it is sorted, cleaned, washed, and dried. Larger pieces, referred to as *pita*, are sometimes sold in markets in Greece. The more common form is small tears that range from 1/8 to 1/2 inch long.

Dried gum mastic is very pale golden-yellow, translucent, and hard. It should be stored in a cool, dry place to prevent it from turning cloudy and losing flavor. The tears can be chewed like chewing gum as a mouth freshener (mastic is used commercially in chewing gums and toothpastes); they will soften and turn bright white and opaque. Mastic's culinary uses in Greece, Turkey, and other eastern Mediterranean countries include desserts such as ice creams, puddings, and cakes, for which it is pounded with sugar, lemon juice, and orange blossom water or rose water, as well as Turkish delight, the popular sweet. It flavors breads, including a Greek festival bread, and some savory dishes, and it is an ingredient in liqueurs such as the eponymous Greek *mastiha*.

MEDICINAL USES: Chewing mastic can soothe an upset stomach. Some practitioners credit mastic with improving liver function, and it has been claimed to help reduce cholesterol levels. It is used as an antiseptic in dentistry.

MELEGUETA PEPPER

See Grains of Paradise.

METHI

See Fenugreek and Fenugreek Seeds.

MIDDLE EASTERN FIVE-SPICE MIX

See Quatre Épices.

MINT

BOTANICAL NAMES: *Mentha spicata/M. crispa/M. viridis* (spearmint);
M. piperata officinalis (peppermint)
FORMS: fresh and dried leaves

There are hundreds of varieties of mint, but spearmint, which is native to Europe and Asia, is the one used most often in the kitchen. It is an ancient perennial, known to the early Greeks and Romans and mentioned in the Bible. Its name comes from the shape of its narrow green leaves, although there is a type of spearmint with rounder leaves. Its fragrance is refreshing, as is its flavor, which is sweet and less pungent than that of many other mints. (All mints contain menthol, the source of the mint flavor.) Peppermint is a more recent variety, dating back to the 1600s and believed to be a cross between spearmint and water mint. Mint self-hybridizes easily, resulting in the dozens of mints found around the world. Peppermint has darker leaves and a stronger

MINT TEA Pour 1 cup boiling water over 1 teaspoon crushed dried mint and steep for 5 minutes. Enjoy hot, or let cool and pour over ice for a refreshing summer drink.

(continued on page 192)

MINT
fresh and dried

menthol flavor than spearmint, and it is more often used for desserts and sweets (as well as for throat lozenges and medicines). Of the other mints of culinary interest are apple mint, which has a milder flavor; pineapple mint (which, confusingly, is sometimes called apple mint), with a slightly fruity taste; and the various citrus mints—as well as chocolate mint, which does have a faint scent of chocolate. (Note that what is called Vietnamese mint, rau ram, is not in fact a mint at all but is instead in the same family as sorrel.)

The fresh mint sold in the market is most often spearmint, and dried mint is usually spearmint as well. Drying the herb seems to concentrate its flavor, though its aroma and taste will dissipate after several months. Dried mint is sometimes referred to as "rubbed" mint, as the leaves are rubbed off the stems once they have dried. Avoid any packages with evident pieces of pale stems.

Mint complements meats such as pork and veal, as well as chicken, and, of course, lamb paired with mint is a classic. But that doesn't have to mean roast lamb with bright green mint jelly— there are delicious mint sauces, and Mediterranean cuisines use mint in marinades and rubs for grilled lamb. Mint flavors many dishes in Morocco and the Middle East. In India, mint chutneys and relishes are very popular, as is a raita made with yogurt, mint, and cucumber. Mint is delicious with buttered steamed potatoes and good in chilled soups like pea or cream of cucumber. Spearmint or peppermint is often added to fruit salads, and mint is a lovely addition to a lemon tart or other citrus dessert. Crème de menthe and other liqueurs are based on mint. Mint green tea is served in almost every household in Morocco, with accompanying ritual, and mint tea (see sidebar, page 190) is a soothing, refreshing drink much loved throughout much of the Middle East, Turkey, and beyond.

MEDICINAL USES: Mint is relatively high in vitamins A and C and a good source of iron, potassium, calcium, and magnesium, among other minerals. Mint tea is often prescribed as a digestive or stimulant.

MUSTARD

BOTANICAL NAMES: *Brassica alba* or *B. hirta, Sinapis alba* (white or yellow); *B. juncea* (brown); *B. nigra* (black)
OTHER NAMES: Chinese mustard, Indian mustard (brown mustard)
FORMS: whole seeds, cracked seeds, and ground

There are three main types of mustard plant, all of which are Brassicas, members of the same family as cabbage and broccoli. White (aka yellow) mustard, the most familiar to Westerners, is probably native to southern Europe and the Mediterranean, but it grows throughout Europe and North America; Canada is one of the largest producers today. (Because the mustard plant now grows in most temperate zones, the precise origins of the three types are subject to some debate.) Brown mustard is indigenous to India and China but is now grown in Great Britain, the United States, and throughout the central latitudes. Black mustard is native to Asia and India; because, unlike white and brown mustard, it is difficult to harvest mechanically, it is grown on a much smaller scale than the other two types. Mustard is an ancient plant—Pliny wrote about its medicinal benefits in first-century Rome, where it was also used as a condiment. It has been cultivated in Europe for centuries, and it was one of the most popular spices in medieval kitchens.

The mustard plant is an annual, and all varieties produce yellow flowers (those of white mustard are bright yellow; brown

(continued on page 195)

mustard flowers are paler); a field of mustard in bloom is a beautiful sight. The white mustard plant is the smallest, reaching about 3 feet; brown and black mustards can grow as tall as 9 feet. The seedpods contain from six to twelve seeds, depending on the variety. The seeds are harvested when the pods have matured but are not fully ripened, as they, especially those of black mustard, can shatter easily if left on the plant longer. The cut plants are then allowed to dry and threshed.

The tiny yellow to pale brown seeds of the white mustard plant are the largest of the three. Unlike other spices, mustard seeds have almost no aroma, because the enzyme that gives mustard its hot, sharp flavor is activated only when it comes into contact with a liquid. Black mustard seeds are the most pungent, followed by the brown and then yellow seeds. (The word *mustard* is believed to have come from the Latin term *mustum ardens,* meaning "burning must.") The brown seeds have a slightly bitter edge. Mustard powder can be made from any type of seeds or a combination. The seeds are finely ground and, for the finest result (also called mustard flour), sifted to remove the husks. Colman's dry mustard powder from England is one of the most highly regarded; it is a blend of finely ground yellow and brown mustard seeds. Cracked mustard seeds are also sometimes available in the market.

Mustard seeds are used in many Indian curries and other dishes. They are usually added at the beginning of cooking, heated in hot oil until they pop before the other seasonings and ingredients go into the pan. Mustard seeds that have been crushed to a paste are used in spicy Bengali marinades and pastes; the seeds are also an ingredient in the Bengali spice blend panch phoron (see page 214). Mustard oil is used in Indian cooking, but it is a neutral oil, not a hot one as you might expect; it is cold-

(continued on next page)

pressed from brown mustard seeds. Ghee or cooking oil that has been infused with the flavor of mustard seeds, as described above, is used as a rub or coating for roasted chicken, beef, or lamb. Whole mustard seeds are used for pickling in many cuisines. When cracked or coarsely ground, they may be added to rubs for grilled or roasted meats. The seeds have an affinity for cabbage, which is not surprising, given that they are members of the same family, and they are often an ingredient in potato salads. Mustard powder is added to many vinaigrettes, both for flavor and to aid emulsification.

To make homemade mustard from mustard powder, always use cold water, not hot, which would kill the enzymes that give mustard its flavor. Add enough water to give you the desired consistency and let stand for 10 minutes to bring out the flavor. The pungency will diminish on standing, so homemade mustard is best used the day it is made. Commercial mustards, of course, remain shelf-stable for months.

MEDICINAL USES: A mustard poultice is a traditional folk remedy, rubbed on the chest to help relieve colds and congestion. Mustard is believed to be a diuretic and a stimulant. It is important in Ayurvedic medicine, said to improve digestion, increase circulation, and ease painful muscles and joints, among many other benefits.

NIGELLA

NUTMEG

NIGELLA

BOTANICAL NAME: *Nigella sativa*
OTHER NAMES: black seed, black onion or black caraway seed
(erroneously), kalongi
FORMS: whole seeds

Nigella is a hardy annual native to western Asia, southern Europe, and the Middle East; it is related to a decorative plant that is often known as "love in a mist." The Romans used nigella seeds in the kitchen, but the spice was better known in ancient Asia for its medicinal properties. Today, nigella is primarily grown in India; it is cultivated to a lesser degree in northern Africa and parts of the Middle East. Its name can be a source of confusion in India, where it is sometimes referred to as black onion or black caraway seed, though it is related to neither; the confusion can also extend to the spice market, where either of those seeds, or sometimes even black sesame seeds, may be identified as nigella.

Each nigella plant has five seedpods, or capsules, which look something like those of the poppy plant. These are harvested just before they ripen fully—as they burst or shatter easily when completely mature—and are dried, then crushed and sifted or threshed to remove the seeds. The tiny black seeds have a distinctive rounded triangular shape. They have a faint peppery aroma and a pungent, nutty, and slightly metallic taste. They are usually used whole but can be ground, preferably in a spice grinder, since they are very hard; for the best results, toast them first, to make them more brittle and easier to grind.

Nigella seeds are often sprinkled onto doughs for Indian naan and for Turkish or Middle Eastern flatbreads. They are

(continued on next page)

also used to season Armenian string cheese and other hard white cheeses. For cooking, they are best either dry-roasted or toasted in oil at the beginning of a dish. In India, they are used to season vegetables or legumes. They can also be added to pickles and chutneys. Nigella seeds are one of the ingredients in the Bengali five-spice mix panch phoron (see page 214).

NUTMEG

BOTANICAL NAME: *Mystica fragrans*
FORMS: whole and ground

Nutmeg is the seed, or kernel, of a tall tropical evergreen tree native to the Moluccas, the Spice Islands. Today, it is also cultivated in Malaysia, Sri Lanka, and the West Indies—Grenada is one of the largest producers—and in the Indian state of Kerala. Nutmeg has long been used for medicinal purposes in China, India, and Arabian countries. By the sixteenth century, it was valued in Europe as both a spice and a curative—and it, as well as mace, was considered an aphrodisiac.

The nutmeg tree is the source of mace as well as of nutmeg (for more about mace, see page 180). The trees start bearing fruit after seven years and remain productive for forty years or longer. The fruits are harvested when ripe, either by simply gathering the fruits that have dropped from the trees or, in some countries, by removing them from the trees with long-handled baskets. The ripe fruits look something like a nectarine or an apricot but are sour and bitter and so are not eaten out of hand; they may be pickled or cooked into preserves. The ripe fruits are split open to

You can certainly grate nutmeg with a Microplane or other sharp grater, but specially designed nutmeg graters are handy—and if you come across an old one in an antique shop, it will make a decorative addition to your kitchen. Long and narrow, shaped like a half cylinder, nutmeg graters usually also have a small compartment for storing whole nutmegs.

reveal the nutmegs wrapped in their lacy covering of mace. The mace is removed and dried separately, and the seeds are dried in the sun until they rattle within their thin outer shells, a process that generally takes four to six weeks. Then the shells are cracked open and the nutmegs removed and graded.

The dried seeds are hard, oval, and pale brown. A cross section of a nutmeg will reveal a pattern of the veins that contain its oil. The seeds are sold whole or ground, but it is better to grate nutmeg yourself before using it, as the oils are volatile and the flavor dissipates quickly once the seeds are ground (see sidebar). The aroma is rich and warm, and the taste is warm and bittersweet.

Nutmeg flavors cakes and other baked goods and creamy desserts such as custard; it's especially good in rice pudding. It is the classic garnish for eggnog, and in Scandinavia, it flavors mulled wine. It is also widely used in savory cooking. In Europe, grated nutmeg is stirred into many vegetable dishes, including mashed potatoes and other vegetable purees; it complements root vegetables particularly well. It also has an affinity for spinach. Nutmeg is the classic seasoning for béchamel sauce and is also

(continued on next page)

good in cheese sauces. In Greece, it seasons moussaka, and in Italy, it is often an ingredient in lasagna. It is also used in charcuterie, as well as in spice mixes in India and the Middle East.

MEDICINAL USES: Nutmeg is known to be a digestive. It has a variety of other applications in traditional Indian and Chinese medicine.

ONION POWDER

See Garlic (and Onion) Powder.

OREGANO

BOTANICAL NAMES: *Origanum vulgare* (Mediterranean); *Lippia graveolens* (Mexican)

OTHER NAMES: (Mediterranean) wild marjoram, Greek oregano, rigani

Mediterranean oregano is a pungent herb native to the Mediterranean region. It's an ancient plant, and its name comes from the Greek for "joy of the mountains," referring to both the fragrance and the beautiful sight of wild oregano blanketing rocky Mediterranean hillsides. A member of the mint family, oregano is actually wild marjoram (see Marjoram, page 187). Many different varieties grow in Greece, where they are collectively referred to as *rigani*.

Oregano is one of the few herbs that most home cooks and chefs alike prefer in its dried state, particularly for tomato and other long-simmered sauces (common marjoram, on the other hand, is more often used as a fresh herb). The aroma remains

(continued on page 207)

OREGANO
dried Mexican and dried Mediterranean

pungent, and the flavor is equally sharp, clean, and warm, with just a slight bitterness. Dried Greek oregano, *rigani,* is often sold packaged still on its long stems, but attractive and aromatic as the bunches are, the leaves should generally be removed from the stems before storing. In either case, crumble or crush the leaves between your fingertips when adding them to the dish you are cooking.

Mediterranean oregano pairs well with marjoram, sage, thyme, basil, and garlic and onions. It is an essential ingredient in Italian cuisine, where it is the defining herb in pizza sauce and many other tomato sauces. It also appears in many Italian herb blends. It complements eggplant, zucchini, and peppers, as well as tomatoes, and it seasons vegetable dishes throughout the region. Oregano is also good in egg and cheese dishes. Combined with other herbs and aromatics, or simply with salt and pepper, the dried herb is used as a rub for grilled or roasted meats, and it seasons meat and vegetable stews. (Oregano is also an ingredient in many chili powders.) In Turkey and various Middle Eastern countries, oregano seasons meat for kebabs and other meat dishes. A favorite herb in Greek cooking, it is used with spit-roasted lamb or kid and in moussaka and fillings for stuffed vegetables. Oregano oil can be drizzled over dishes as a finishing touch or used as a simple rub for meats and poultry.

The equally pungent Mexican oregano, or *orégano,* is not related to the Mediterranean herb, although it is often mistakenly believed to be the same species. Mexican oregano is actually a shrub in the verbena family, and its leaves are larger than the Mediterranean variety. (Confusingly, there is a type of oregano grown in Mexico that is in the same family as Mediterranean oregano, and there are various other herbs or plants that may be referred to as

(continued on next page)

oregano there.) Mexican oregano is native to South America but is now primarily grown in Mexico (in other Latin American countries, it is more often Mediterranean oregano that is cultivated today). The aroma and flavor of Mexican oregano will be familiar, but it has a noticeable citrus character, like lemon verbena. It, too, can be used as a rub for grilled or roasted meats. In Mexico, it is an ingredient in moles and other sauces, in stews, and in soups such as pozole, and it may be added to long-simmered bean dishes. It can also be used to season Tex-Mex dishes such as chili, and is commonly found in the brine of pickled jalapeños.

MEDICINAL USES: Mediterranean oregano is high in antioxidants and in vitamins A, C, and K. Essential oregano oil is prescribed for a variety of ailments, and oregano can be brewed into a tea to soothe coughs or an upset stomach.

ORRIS ROOT

BOTANICAL NAME: *Iris germanica* L. v. *florentina, I. pallida*
OTHER NAMES: Florentine iris
FORMS: coarsely chopped and ground dried rhizomes

Orris root comes come from the underground rhizome of the flowering Florentine iris. The varieties most often used for culinary orris root are indigenous to the countries of the eastern Mediterranean.

Once the plants have matured, the rhizomes are harvested, peeled, and dried, then finely chopped or, more often, finely ground. Orris root is very aromatic, and the flavor is bittersweet and pungent, even peppery. The fine powder is pale yellow;

chopped bits of dried orris root are a mix of light brown and white.

Orris root was widely used in sixteenth- and seventeenth-century kitchens, but its popularity as a cooking ingredient has dwindled since then, and today its main role is in the perfumery industry or for spice sachets and the like. As such, it is now more of a culinary curiosity, but it remains a defining ingredient in the Moroccan spice blend ras el hanout (see page 248). It is still used in some regional dishes in other southern Mediterranean countries and for some liqueurs, including a type of Spanish bitters.

MEDICINAL USES: Orris root has various folk medicine applications and is sometimes used for "detoxes," infused into a tea.

PANCH PHORON

OTHER NAMES: panch phora, panch puran, Bengali five-spice mix

Panch phoron is an essential seasoning in Bengali cooking and is used in some other northern Indian cuisines as well. *Panch* means "five," and *phoron* means "seeds," and the mix consists of cumin, fenugreek, mustard, nigella, and fennel seeds. The proportions vary—some mixes include equal parts of all five seeds, others are made with different amounts to taste. Panch phoron is sold as whole seeds or ground; some cooks like to use crushed whole seeds. The whole-seed blend is an attractive, colorful mix, with its black nigella, yellow fenugreek, black or brown mustard, greenish-gray cumin, and pale green fennel seeds. Whether it is whole or ground, the mix is intensely aromatic and the flavor pungent.

Panch phoron is often fried in oil or ghee at the beginning of a recipe for a flavoring base, but it is also used as a finishing touch, heated in ghee that is then poured over the dish just before serving. It complements lentils and other legumes and is a seasoning in many dals, as well as in fish, meat, and vegetable curries and other dishes. Panch phoron can be used as a pickling spice, and some chutneys include it. It pairs particularly well with starches such as potatoes. Sometimes the coarsely cracked spices are sprinkled over a flatbread or other bread dough before baking.

PANCH PHORON

top plate: black mustard seeds; *right plate:*
fenugreek, cumin; *bottom plate, clockwise from
top:* nigella, fenugreek, and fennel seeds

PANDAN LEAVES

BOTANICAL NAME: *Pandanus amaryllifolius*
OTHER NAMES: screwpine, pandanus, daun pandan, bai toey, rampe
FORMS: fresh and sliced or ground dried leaves

Pandan leaves come from the screwpine tree, a tall ancient tree that is native to Southeast Asia and Madagascar (despite its name, it is not a pine tree). The leaves are long and sword shaped and have a variety of traditional uses beyond the kitchen, from thatching roofs to being woven into sails or mats. The small woven baskets in which sticky rice is served in many Asian restaurants are often made with pandan leaves. The leaves are also used to wrap rice before steaming it or cooking it on a grill.

Pandan leaves are called *daun pandan* in Indonesia and Malaysia, *bai toey* or *bai toey hom* in Thailand, and *rampe* in Sri Lanka and India. The large leaves are carefully dried to preserve their color and then sliced or chopped into large pieces or ground to a fine powder. The leaves have a sweet, grassy, slightly nutty aroma and a subtly floral, sweetish taste. The fragrant powder should be a striking green color; paler powders are older and should be avoided.

Pandan leaves are used in both sweet and savory dishes in Thai, Vietnamese, Malaysian, Indonesian, and other Southeast Asian cuisines. They flavor many rice dishes, soups, and stews; if added as large pieces, they are removed before serving. A popular sponge cake is flavored with pandan, giving it a shocking green color that looks artificial but is in fact natural, and pandan

PANDAN TEA Pour 1 cup boiling water over 2 to 3 tablespoons chopped dried pandan leaves and steep for 3 to 5 minutes, then strain.

is sometimes added to rice pudding. It can also be infused into a tea (see sidebar, opposite). *Kewra,* an essence derived from the flowers of the screwpine tree, has a delicate floral flavor and is an ingredient in Indian sweets and drinks, as well as in some savory dishes, including pulaos.

PAPRIKA

BOTANICAL NAME: *Capsicum annum*
OTHER NAMES: pimentón
FORMS: ground

Although Hungarian paprika is more familiar to most people, it was actually the Spanish who first produced the powder, after Columbus and other explorers brought chile peppers back to Spain from Mexico. Paprika is in the nightshade family, and there are many different varieties of the plant, bearing fruits of different shapes and sizes. Some of them look like small bell peppers, others are heart shaped, and still others look like long thin chiles; most are low on the Scoville heat scale (see page 57). The main sources of paprika today are Hungary and Spain, but Israel, Portugal, Morocco, and the United States are also notable producers.

Paprika peppers are always harvested when ripe and red. They are dried and cured, then ground. Hotter paprikas usually include varying amounts of the seeds and ribs, while some of the best sweet paprikas contain none of these at all. Paprika is graded according to the proportions of seeds, ribs, and/or stems it contains, as well as the fineness of the grind and the quality of the final product.

Most Hungarian paprika is either hot or sweet. Sweet paprikas are bright red; hotter ones tend to have a slightly darker

(continued on page 219)

color. Paprika gives Hungarian goulash its signature flavor, and it is used in many other dishes, including chicken paprikash. It is an amalgamating spice and complements most other spices and many herbs, from allspice and cloves to rosemary and sage. It is an ingredient in numerous spice blends and commercial seasoning blends, including chili powders and dry rubs for grilled meat and chicken. Of course, classic deviled eggs are always finished with a sprinkling of paprika.

Pimentón is the Spanish word for "paprika," and although Spain does produce "regular" paprika, of more culinary interest is smoked pimentón, made from peppers that have been slowly smoked over wood fires, giving it a distinctive aroma and flavor. The best pimentón comes from La Vera in Extremadura, and it has been awarded DOP status and labeled accordingly with "Denominación de Origen Protegida"; any pimentón from La Vera will include that on the label as well. There are three types of pimentón: *picante* (hot), *dulce* (sweet), and *agridulce* (bittersweet). Pimentón is added to many soups and stews and is used in *patatas bravas,* a favorite tapa of fried potatoes, where it can season both the potatoes themselves and the accompanying tomato sauce (other versions of *patatas bravas* are served with allioli, the garlicky mayonnaise, and it too can be seasoned with pimentón). A similar Middle Eastern dish is *batata harra.* Pimentón is an essential ingredient in Spanish chorizo, and it can be added to a spice rub to season grilled meat, especially pork, or poultry.

PARSLEY

BOTANICAL NAMES: *Petroselinum crispum* (curly); *P. crispum neapolitanum* (flat-leaf)
OTHER NAMES: Italian parsley (flat-leaf)
FORMS: fresh and dried or freeze-dried leaves

Parsley grows abundantly in so many regions that its origins have become blurred, but most sources describe it as indigenous to southern Europe and the eastern Mediterranean. Its botanical name, *Petroselinum,* is derived from the Greek word for stone, *petro,* because it could often be seen growing on the rocky hillsides of that country. There are two main types of parsley, curly and flat-leaf, and many subspecies. The leaves of curly parsley are tightly furled; those of flat-leaf are darker green and look somewhat like celery leaves. Curly parsley was originally the type found in most markets in the United States, but now flat-leaf, which has a slightly stronger and more appealing flavor, is commonly available as well. Dried parsley, which is usually curly parsley, retains its flavor surprisingly well; it should be deep green, without noticeable bits of stalk.

Because of the herb's ubiquitous use as a garnish, the versatility of parsley, one of the most important members of the Apiaceae (formerly Umbelliferae) family, is sometimes taken for granted. It has a clean green flavor and complements a wide variety of other herbs, both pungent and mild. It is used in cuisines around the world, wherever the climate is temperate. (Parsley is a perennial and can winter over, but it is often treated as an annual because the taste of the leaves from the second season can be a bit harsher.) Fresh parsley is part of persillade, a classic French seasoning mixture of finely chopped parsley and garlic, and of Italy's

(continued on page 222)

gremolata, a combination of minced parsley, garlic, and lemon zest that is the traditional garnish for osso buco. It is one of the three herbs in any bouquet garni (see page 36), and it is part of many herb blends. It is an essential ingredient in tabbouleh, the Middle Eastern herb salad made with bulgur wheat; the authentic version is really a parsley salad, not a grain salad, as so often seems to be the case.

Parsley seasons many stews, braises, soups, and other long-cooked dishes. It complements most vegetables, including root vegetables, and *pommes de terre persillées,* boiled new potatoes with parsley and butter, are traditionally served with simple fish dishes in France. Parsley is added to many sauces for seafood, chicken, or meats. It is also good with both egg and cheese dishes. In short, it is widely used for good reason.

PEPPER

BOTANICAL NAME: *Piper nigrum*
FORMS: whole peppercorns and ground

Black, white, green, and true pink peppercorns are all the fruits of a climbing vine that is native to southern India. Several relatives and one "imposter" are described in detail on the following pages, along with two types of Asian pepper. Pepper is often called the king of spices, and it dominated and determined the history of the spice trade for centuries. Pepper, specifically long pepper (see page 231), was mentioned in Sanskrit writings as early as 1000 BC. Black pepper eventually gained ascendancy over long pepper—at one time, it was actually worth its weight in gold. During the Middle Ages, salaries and rents were sometimes paid in peppercorns.

FOLLOWING SPREAD, FROM LEFT TO RIGHT, TOP ROW: Tellicherry, green, Penja, and Sarawak; MIDDLE ROW: Szechuan (crushed), pink, and cubeb; BOTTOM ROW: Wynad, Szechuan (whole berries), Muntok, and long

Today, India remains one of the major sources of pepper, along with Malaysia and Indonesia; Brazil is also a major producer.

Piper nigrum is a perennial vine that can grow to as high as 30 feet, though the plants on spice plantations are generally much shorter. In India, the plants are trained to grow up trees; elsewhere, they may be grown on trellises. The vines, which can take eight years to reach maturity, will bear fruit for up to twenty years after that. They have large, shiny, dark green leaves, and the peppercorns, also called berries, grow in long clusters, or spikes, of up to fifty fruits. Peppercorns are always harvested by hand, and the clusters of berries on each plant do not all reach maturity at once, so harvesting is repeated over time until all the clusters have been picked.

Black peppercorns are harvested when they have reached their full size but are still green and are dried in the sun for days, until they turn black and wrinkled. Green peppercorns are usually picked earlier than the berries destined for black pepper and treated in various ways to preserve their color; see page 229. White peppercorns, which are picked when slightly riper than those for black pepper, are traditionally produced by removing the outer husks (the pericarp) before drying the berries. A more modern technique removes the husks from dried black peppercorns mechanically, but the results are not as good as with the older methods, which are still used by better producers. Real pink peppercorns (see Pink Pepper, page 229) are berries that have been allowed to ripen fully and then preserved in brine. The ripe berries do not stand up to other

(continued on page 226)

methods of preservation, including freeze-drying, and true pink pepper is rarely seen in the market.

Black peppercorns have a warm, pungent fragrance and equally pungent flavor and heat. White pepper tastes hotter and sharper than black, and the less mature green pepper berries have a fresher taste and less heat. Pepper is always best when freshly ground; preground pepper has far less pungency and flavor. Good pepper mills are not expensive and are well worth the investment. Or, if you need a large amount of freshly ground black pepper, use a spice grinder.

BLACK AND WHITE PEPPER

LAMPONG: Lampong pepper comes from the Lampung province of Sumatra in Indonesia (the name of the province is properly spelled Lampung, but for some reason, the peppercorns are usually referred to as "Lampong"). The berries are smaller than many other peppercorns and intensely aromatic, with a slight citrusy perfume and notes of pine. Their fragrance is stronger than their flavor, which is mildly pungent, with lingering heat.

MALABAR: Malabar pepper comes from India's Malabar Coast (as does Tellicherry pepper; see page 228) and is considered of very high quality. It is sometimes called Alleppey pepper, after the region that is the source of much of the pepper. Malabar peppercorns have a rich, woodsy aroma and a pungent flavor, with a good amount of heat; they are used in many spice mixes, as well as for everyday cooking.

MUNTOK: Muntok is an Indonesian pepper from the island of Bangka; the vines grow on the hills above the village of Muntok.

Most white peppercorns in the market are of the Muntok variety. To make Muntok white pepper, the berries are soaked in water to remove their dark outer layer; once it has been removed, some of the peppercorns remain mottled or darker than others in the batch. Traditionally, the spikes of the plant were packed into empty rice sacks and soaked in a stream to loosen the outer shells, then mounded into piles for the *nari mereca* (pepper dance), wherein the villagers would tramp on them to remove the berries from the spikes before the peppers were dried and bleached in the sun. Muntok pepper has a winy, somewhat creamy flavor and complements fish and seafood well.

PENJA: Penja pepper is a rare variety that comes from the Penja Valley in Cameroon, where the vines thrive in the region's rich volcanic soil. The black peppercorns are actually a very dark brown, fragrant, and quite spicy, with a heat that builds and lingers on the tongue. The white peppercorns have a warm, bold flavor, stronger than that of most other white peppers, and many chefs and other connoisseurs prefer Penja white pepper. It is especially good with fish and seafood, eggs, and creamy sauces.

SARAWAK: This Malaysian pepper, from Sarawak, on the island of Borneo, is considered one of the best, especially since its quality has improved in recent years. It has a fruity aroma and a slight sweetness. Its mild heat makes it suited to a variety of uses, even sweet dishes such as custards and fruit desserts. Many spice merchants find this to be their most popular peppercorn.

Sarawak is also sold as white pepper. The berries are soaked in running mountain streams to remove the dark outer layer, and the resulting peppercorns have a uniform creamy white color.

(continued on next page)

TELLICHERRY: Tellicherry is a very high-quality Malabar pepper, from India's southwestern coast (see Malabar, above). The berries are larger than most, and they have a robust, almost fruity aroma. Tellicherry peppercorns have only moderate heat, but the flavor is intense, with lovely citrus notes. It is the favorite peppercorn of many spice lovers.

VIETNAMESE: Few people are familiar with Vietnamese pepper, though they may indeed have tasted it, since in the last decade or so, Vietnam has become the world's largest producer and exporter of the spice. Its aroma is quite pungent and its flavor is complex, even exotic, with citrusy, fruity notes and undertones of smokiness, or of smoky tea. Its heat is fairly moderate.

WYNAD: This is a specialty pepper produced at the Parameswaran plantation on the Wynad Plateau in Kerala, India, a region that has long been known for the quality of its peppercorns. Unlike other berries, which are harvested when green and unripe, these are left on the vine until red and fully ripened, which results in an intense and unique flavor (and it also makes the harvest more difficult, since green peppercorns can be picked all at once, while waiting for the peppercorns to fully ripen results in several harvests over a period of time). The peppercorns are then sun-dried and packaged. The Parameswaran plantation is the only one currently producing and exporting this pepper (they also produce white pepper); it's not surprising that it is more expensive than most, but chefs and pepper lovers rave about it. The flavor is complex and the heat level fairly subtle. Coarsely grind or crush it and use it for *steak au poivre,* or add a little of it to regular pepper for *cacio e pepe,* the Roman pasta dish made with sheep's-milk cheese and lots of black pepper.

GREEN PEPPER

Green peppercorns are unripe pepper berries that are treated in one of several different ways to preserve their green color; if they were simply air-dried or dried in the sun, they would turn black. Depending on the producer, they may be picked a few weeks or so before pepper berries that will be dried to black pepper are; in any case, the berries have reached full size but have not begun to ripen. Traditionally, green peppercorns were pickled in brine or vinegar to preserve the color, and brine- or vinegar-packed green peppercorns are readily available today. They are of good quality but usually need to be rinsed before using. A more modern preservation technique is freeze-drying (keep in mind that freeze-dried peppercorns are very light in weight, so they may seem much more expensive than other dried peppercorns, but you are getting more peppercorns ounce per ounce); these reconstitute quickly in liquid. And more recently, some producers have found it possible to successfully air-dry (or sun-dry) green peppercorns by first blanching or soaking them briefly in brine or vinegar, which preserves their color.

Green peppercorns are mildly piquant and have an appealing fresh flavor. They are used in dishes such as *steak au poivre vert*, with its delicious cream sauce, and in terrines, pâtés, and other charcuterie. Crush or grind the dried peppercorns just before using them, to preserve their fragrance and flavor. Green pepper is part of most peppercorn mixes.

PINK PEPPER

So-called pink peppercorns are not actually related to true peppercorns at all; they are a member of the *Schinus terebinthifolius* or *S. mole* family, rather than *Piper nigrum*. (Real peppercorns do turn red when fully ripened, but these are rarely seen.) The berries come

(continued on next page)

from a tree, sometimes called the pepper tree or the Christmas berry tree, that is native to the Andes; it is in the same family as the mastic tree (see page 188). Most of the pink pepper on the market today comes from the French island of Réunion, in the Indian Ocean. The peppercorns are sold dried, in brine, or freeze-dried, and they are included in many peppercorn blends. They have a peppery fragrance but a somewhat sweet flavor. Their papery outer husks are brittle and flake off easily, revealing the hard seed within. The flavor is somewhat fleeting, and they are sometimes used as a garnish rather than a seasoning. They add both visual appeal and a delicate taste to fish dishes, and they complement game such as venison.

CUBEB PEPPER

Cubeb pepper comes from another vine in the pepper family, *Piper cubeb*. It is native to Indonesia, and although it was used in European kitchens in the Middle Ages, it is little known in the West today. It has been used in China and other parts of Asia for medicinal as well as culinary purposes since ancient times. The berries are harvested when still green and dried in the sun. The dried berries have little "tails," and tailed pepper is another name for cubeb. The dried peppercorns are dark brown, with some tails still intact. When cracked open, the berries have a distinct aroma of turpentine. The flavor, though, is warm and pungent, with notes of ginger and allspice; in fact, some people find the flavor closer to allspice than to pepper. Cubeb pepper is used mostly in the cooking of Indonesia (though it remains important in Eastern medicine). It is also an ingredient in many versions of ras el hanout, the Moroccan seasoning blend (see page 248).

LONG PEPPER

Long pepper, *Piper longum,* is native to India. It is sometimes called Indian pepper, and its Sanskrit name, *pippali,* is the origin of both the Latin (*piper*) and English words for pepper. Long pepper was known to the ancient Greeks and Romans before black pepper, and it has a long history in Asia. Long pepper berries, or buds, are harvested when still green and dried in the sun. They are usually 1 to 1½ inches long and resemble small grayish-brown pinecones (one of their other names is peppercones) or tiny cattails. The dried peppercorns have a strong aroma of ginger and the taste is peppery and slightly sweet; when chewed, long pepper has a numbing effect. Today, long pepper is used primarily in India, Indonesia, and Malaysia, where it seasons curries, soups, and a variety of other dishes and is often added to pickles or preserves. It is also an ingredient in some versions of ras el hanout (see page 248).

SZECHUAN PEPPER

Szechuan peppercorns are the berries of a small prickly ash tree (*Zanthoxylum simulans*) native to China; Szechuan pepper is not related to black pepper. Its Chinese name is *fagara,* and it is also sometimes called Chinese pepper or anise pepper. The berries are harvested when ripe, dried in the sun until they split open, and cleaned or sifted. They are very aromatic, warm and peppery, with a pronounced citrus fragrance (the prickly ash tree is a member of the citrus family). The taste is spicy, peppery, and sharp. Culinary authority Harold McGee writes that sanshools, the pungent compounds found in both Szechuan and sansho pepper (see page 232), are in the same family as capsaicin, which gives chiles their heat, and piperine, found in black pepper. "But," he says,

(continued on next page)

"the sanshools aren't simply pungent. They produce a strange tingling, buzzing, numbing sensation that is something like the effect of carbonated drinks or a mild electrical current!"

The prickly ash tree has sharp thorns, and sometimes a few of these will be found in the package, as will some longer stems, so be sure to pick over the peppercorns before using them. The inner seeds are gritty when ground and can be bitter; discard any that have collected at the bottom of the package, and, if you desire, shake more of them out of the split berries. The berries are often toasted before using; they can be added whole to a dish or crushed or ground. The ground pepper loses its fragrance quickly, so it's best to buy whole peppercorns and crush or grind them yourself before use. Szechuan pepper is one of the ingredients in Chinese five-spice powder (see page 79), and it pairs well with ginger and star anise. It is an essential seasoning in Szechuan cooking and in other regional cuisines, used in dishes from mapo tofu to roast chicken. It can also be part of a spice rub for grilled or roasted meats and fish. Coarse sea salt ground with toasted Szechuan pepper is a popular seasoning in China, and Szechuan pepper oil, made by heating oil with peppercorns to infuse it with their flavor and then straining it, is used as a cooking oil or to dress salads and vegetables.

Sansho pepper comes from a prickly ash that is cultivated in Japan, *Zanthoxylum piperitum,* and is a close relative of *Z. simulans.* The berries are dried and cleaned in a similar way, but sansho pepper is more likely to be sold ground to a greenish-yellow powder. It is milder than Szechuan pepper, with pronounced notes of citrus, but it produces the same tingling, numbing sensation. In Japan, sansho is used to season fatty foods like eel and duck; it may also be sprinkled over a dish before serving (the tins or jars of pepper

(continued on page 235)

SZECHUAN PEPPERCORNS

usually have shaker tops). It is one of the ingredients in shichimi togarashi, the Japanese spice blend (see page 279).

PICKLING SPICES

OTHER NAMES: pickling spice

Pickling spices are used in many cuisines, and the blends vary widely, from simple to complex. The spices, which are usually left whole but are sometimes coarsely ground, may include mustard seeds, peppercorns, allspice, cloves, celery seeds, dill seeds, bay leaves, ginger, and/or cinnamon. Some blends also include dried chiles or cayenne. A general guideline is to use 1 tablespoon of the spice mix per 1 quart brine. Pickling spices are also used in chutneys and, ground or left whole, to season various dishes or infusions. A version made with chiles can be used as the spice for a crab or other seafood boil.

PIGWEED

See Epazote.

PIMENTÓN

See Paprika.

PIRI PIRI

OTHER SPELLINGS: piri piri, peri peri, pili pili

The term *piri piri* has several different spellings and several different meanings. Piri piri chiles (see page 71) are small, very hot bird peppers grown in Mozambique, but piri piri can also refer to a very hot African spice blend (as here) or a hot sauce or paste. A basic dried blend is made with ground dried chiles, paprika, and sometimes dried lemon peel; some blends may also include oregano or other herbs, as well as dried garlic and onion. The spice mix can be combined with oil, garlic, and lemon juice to make a marinade for grilled chicken, considered by some to be the national dish of Mozambique; the same marinade is also used for meat or seafood. (Piri piri chiles are much loved in Portugal—brought there from Mozambique and Angola by Portuguese explorers—and *frango com piri piri,* grilled chicken with hot sauce, is sold at roadside stands and street stalls all over the country.) The spice blend can also be used as a dry rub for grilled meat, poultry, or shrimp or other seafood or mixed with olive oil for a seasoning for grilled vegetables.

POPPY SEEDS

BOTANICAL NAME: *Papaver somniferum*
OTHER NAMES: maw
FORMS: whole and ground

The poppy plant is an annual native to the Middle East, grown for culinary and medicinal purposes since ancient times. It was used by the early Egyptians, Greeks, and Romans (it was mentioned

(continued on page 238)

POPPY SEEDS
white and black poppy seeds

by Homer), and it has been cultivated in India and China for thousands of years. Major producers today include Holland, France, Canada, India, China, Turkey, and Iran; the plants are also grown in Australia, particularly on the island of Tasmania, and in Southeast Asia.

The plant's botanical name means "sleep-inducing" (remember the poppy-field scene in *The Wizard of Oz*?), because it is the source of opium, as well as of morphine and codeine, but the seeds have no traces of those alkaloids. Opium comes from the latex, or sap, of the unripe seedpods. As the plants mature, the large oval pods become filled with thousands of tiny seeds, contained within several chambers. Once the seed capsules are ripe and have turned yellowish-brown, the plants are harvested and dried before they are cracked and the seeds retrieved.

The more familiar blue, or black, poppy seeds are tiny and hard, and they weigh almost nothing—a pound contains more than a half million seeds. Yellow, or white, poppy seeds, which are common in India, are even smaller. The lesser-known brown seeds come primarily from Turkey. Poppy seeds have a slight nutty fragrance—the blue seeds tend to be slightly more aromatic than the white—that is stronger if they are toasted or otherwise heated and/or ground. The seeds have a high oil content and can turn rancid quickly; store them tightly sealed in a cool place or in the freezer. Poppy seed oil has a variety of uses. The oil from the first cold pressing is a mild oil that can be used in salads and other dishes (later pressings yield an oil that can be further processed and used in artists' paints).

In Europe and North America, poppy seeds are most often used in baking—for cakes, cookies, and crackers—and in confectionery. The seeds pair well with lemon and other citrus fruits, and lemon poppy seed cake is a favorite. And, of course, they are a popular bagel topping. They are also added to coleslaw, as well as to potatoes, vegetables, and pasta and noodle dishes, either as an ingredient or a final garnish. In India (where the seeds are known as *khas-khas* or *kus-kus*) and the Middle East, the seeds are sprinkled over naan and other flatbreads. They are also ground with other spices to flavor and thicken Indian meat, fish, and shellfish curries and other preparations. In Turkey, they are ground into a paste with poppy seed oil to fill or flavor pastries; they are also used there to make halvah.

MEDICINAL USES: In ancient times, poppy seeds were considered a curative for cholera, among other diseases, and they have traditionally been prescribed for dysentery. They are also recommended for other types of intestinal ills. The seeds are rich in omega-3 fatty acids and relatively high in calcium; they are also high in oleic and linoleic fatty acids.

POUDRE DE COLOMBO

See Colombo.

POPPY SEEDS

QÂLAT DAQQA

See Tunisian Five-Spice Mix.

QUATRE ÉPICES

OTHER NAMES: French four-spice mix

Quatre épices is a classic French spice mix, but the actual mix may vary from cook to cook—and from the savory kitchen to the sweet one. And while some blends are made with just four (*quatre*) spices, others may contain five or even more. A typical mix is black or white peppercorns, nutmeg, cloves, and ginger, all ground to a fine powder; some include cinnamon in addition to these or instead of the cloves. Both cinnamon and allspice appear in blends used for baking. Quatre épices is an important seasoning for charcuterie, from sausages to pâtés to terrines. It is also added to beef or game stews, braises, and other long-cooked dishes. Many recipes for *pain d'épices,* a traditional loaf cake sometimes described as the French version of gingerbread, call for quatre épices. The mixture is also used in some Middle Eastern cuisines. A similar blend called Middle Eastern five-spice consists of allspice, peppercorns, cloves, nutmeg, and cinnamon.

R

RADHUNI

BOTANICAL NAMES: *Trachyspermum roxbrughianum, Carum roxburghianum*
OTHER NAMES: wild celery, ajmud, ajmod
FORMS: whole seeds

A member of the same family as celery and parsley, radhuni is thought to be native to India and Southeast Asia, where it is widely grown today. It has been important in Ayurvedic medicine since ancient times.

The tiny greenish-gray seeds are featherlight, oval, and flattish, with a ridge running down one side. The aroma recalls parsley, and the taste is similar to that of celery. Radhuni is also related to ajowan (see page 5), but the taste is milder. Radhuni seeds resemble celery seeds and are often confused with them—but as the two seeds have a similar flavor, they can, in fact, be used interchangeably in many recipes. The flavor intensifies when the seeds are crushed, which can be done easily with a mortar and pestle, or even between your fingertips.

Radhuni seeds are popular in Bengali cuisine but little used in other Indian regions; *radhuni* is the Bengali name. They are often fried in oil until they crackle and become aromatic and then drizzled over dals or other dishes as a finishing touch. Rad-

(continued on next page)

RADHUNI

huni seeds are also used in marinades and pickles, and in certain versions of the favorite Bengali spice blend panch phoron (see page 214).

MEDICINAL USES: In India, radhuni seeds are believed to help respiratory health and relieve liver ailments.

RAS EL HANOUT

Ras el hanout is a Moroccan spice blend that is used across North Africa. *Ras* means "king," and the name is translated as "head of the shop." Vendors at the spice bazaars are often judged by the quality of their ras el hanout. The blends usually contain at least twenty ingredients, although the number can go as high as fifty, and the exact components and ratios are often highly guarded secrets. Ras el hanout mixes are very aromatic, with a floral fragrance, and the flavor is robust but nuanced. Traditionally, they were sold as whole-spice mixes at spice markets, where they could be ground to order, but ground blends are common today. A typical mix may contain coriander, green cardamom, black pepper, cinnamon, ginger, nutmeg, turmeric, cumin, anise, and fennel seeds, as well as dried rosebuds or petals and lavender blossoms. More complicated mixes include spices such as cloves, nigella, cubeb or long pepper, paprika, and/or saffron. Traditional Moroccan versions of ras el hanout always contain ingredients thought to be aphrodisiacs, typically Spanish fly, and sometimes hashish, though you won't find these in any blends sold in the United States! The fragrance is warm, very aromatic, and complex.

(continued on page 250)

RAS EL HANOUT
coriander, green cardamom, black pepper, cinnamon, ginger, nutmeg, turmeric, cumin, anise, fennel seeds, rosebuds, allspice, and lavender

Ras el hanout is used to season everything from couscous and rice dishes to tagines, soups, and stews. It can be used as a dry rub for grilled lamb, beef, chicken, or fish or added to the meat for kebabs. It also flavors the Moroccan sweet called *majoun,* which is made with nuts, dried fruit, honey, and hashish.

RIGANI

See Oregano.

ROSEBUDS

BOTANICAL NAME: *Rosa* spp.

The dried rosebuds sold for culinary uses come from many different varieties of the plant. Although they are most often steeped in boiling water to make a soothing herbal tea, they are also an ingredient in several important Middle Eastern spice blends, most notably ras el hanout (see page 248), as well as advieh (see page 4), a Persian mix, and some North African versions of baharat (see page 24). Look for dried rosebuds with good color and fragrance.

ROSEMARY

BOTANICAL NAME: *Rosmarinus officinalis*
FORMS: fresh and whole or ground dried leaves

Rosemary is a perennial shrub in the mint family that is native to the Mediterranean. Its Latin name, from the words *ros* and *marinus,* translates as "dew of the sea," and it thrives in coastal Mediterra-

(continued on page 252)

ROSEMARY
ground, fresh, and dried

nean regions. It is an ancient herb, known for its medicinal as well as culinary uses since early times. Many myths and legends, some religious, have been associated with rosemary, and in *Hamlet,* Ophelia utters the words, "There's rosemary, that's for remembrance," a sentiment that has been widely repeated.

There are a number of varieties of rosemary, but *Rosmarinus officinalis,* an upright shrub that can reach 5 feet, is probably the most common; a low-growing plant known as *Rosmarinus officinalis 'Prostratus'* is also widely grown. The aroma and flavor are pungent, with piney, minty notes and an undertone of camphor or eucalyptus. The dried leaves, or needles, retain their pungency well, with the same warm, woody characteristics; crush or chop them before using. Preground rosemary is also available, but whole dried leaves are more aromatic and flavorful. Rosemary is a classic flavoring for lamb, often in combination with garlic, and it is good with most grilled or roasted meats, and in marinades for the same. It complements game such as venison, and it flavors pâtés and charcuterie. Rosemary pairs well with other herbs, particularly Mediterranean herbs such as oregano, sage, savory, and thyme, and it is part of the French blend herbes de Provence (see page 145). It is an essential ingredient in classic cassoulet. Breads and crackers can be flavored with rosemary, and it has a place in the sweet kitchen as well, in desserts such as crème brûlée and in shortbread. It is also added to preserves such as apple or citrus jellies.

PREVIOUS SPREAD, CLOCKWISE FROM BOTTOM LEFT: winter savory; saffron; star anise, sambar powder, salam leaves (ON PLATE); sage; ground sumac; sesame seeds; shichimi togarashi; summer savory; and sumac berries

SAFFRON

BOTANICAL NAME: *Crocus sativus*
FORMS: threads and ground

The most expensive spice in the world, saffron comes from a species of crocus believed to be native to Asia Minor and Greece. Its history extends back at least to the tenth century BC. It has been known in most of the countries surrounding the Mediterranean since ancient times, used as a spice and a dye as well as for its medicinal benefits. It was prized by Phoenician traders and by the Greeks, Romans, and Egyptians, and it is mentioned in the Old Testament. Saffron has been cultivated in India for centuries, and India is one of the major producers today, along with Spain and Iran.

Saffron is the dried stigmas of the crocus flower, and it takes more than one hundred thousand flowers to produce one pound of saffron. Each flower has only three stigmas, and these are attached at the bottom of the flower with a pale thread that is called a style. Harvesting saffron is a demanding, painstaking process. The harvest is in the fall, and the flowers are picked early in the morning, to avoid the heat of the sun. Then the stigmas are removed by hand, traditionally by all the women, young and old, of the town. Still attached to the style, the stigmas are then dried, often still over charcoal or in the sun, the traditional methods.

Most grades of saffron will have some of the styles attached; very high-quality versions have had the styles removed. Because of the cost (the price of saffron can be close to half of that of gold by weight), both whole threads and ground saffron have been known to be adulterated—safflower stigmas, the most likely culprit, look somewhat similar but have none of the flavor of the real thing. Dried saffron stigmas are red or red-orange, and the styles are lighter; the deeper the color of the threads, the better. Ground saffron is also marketed, but it is preferable to buy the whole threads and pulverize them at home, both for their fresher flavor and because of the possibility of the preground version being adulterated. Saffron has a distinctive musky, woody fragrance and a pungent, bitter taste. The best Spanish saffron, or *azafrán,* comes from La Mancha, and some believe this is the best in the world, but saffron from Kashmir in India is also very good, as is some of the saffron from Iran.

Saffron's color is water-soluble, and it adds a beautiful yellow tone as well as its flavor to a wide variety of dishes. Spain's paella is one of the most notable of these, along with Italy's *risotto alla Milanese* and France's bouillabaisse, the traditional seafood stew; it also flavors *zarzuela,* the Spanish version of that classic. Fortunately, only a pinch is necessary for most recipes (and too much can add a bitter taste, so it should always be used sparingly). The threads are usually soaked in warm water or another liquid to soften them and bring out the color and then added, with the liquid, to the pot; ground saffron can be added directly to a dish as it cooks. In India, saffron seasons rice and chicken, as well as rich Moghul-style preparations, and it flavors sweet custards and yogurt drinks or desserts. In England, the spice was cultivated in Essex in the

(continued on next page)

Middle Ages, and it is still used in Britain to make traditional saffron cakes. Chartreuse and some other liqueurs are flavored with saffron. It is also used in a traditional Persian stew called *koresh* and a rice dish called *polow.*

MEDICINAL USES: Saffron is traditionally prescribed for digestive and urinary tract disorders, coughs, and asthma.

SAGE

BOTANICAL NAME: *Salvia officinalis*
FORMS: fresh and rubbed or ground dried leaves

Sage, another member of the mint family, is a perennial shrub that is indigenous to the Mediterranean coastal regions of southern Europe; today the best is said to come from Dalmatia, in Croatia, and garden sage is sometimes called Dalmatian sage. There are many varieties, but most have fuzzy green or greenish-gray leaves. Sage is one of the most aromatic of the Mediterranean herbs, with a warm, pungent fragrance and a fresh, strong, even somewhat medicinal taste. Its Latin name comes from the word *salver,* which means "to save" or "to heal," and sage was prized for its medicinal properties for centuries before it became a favorite culinary herb. It was known to the ancient Greeks and Romans, and in the Middle Ages, tea made with sage was prescribed for many ills all around the Mediterranean; the Chinese were also enamored of Europe's sage tea.

When sage is dried, its taste becomes, if anything, more concentrated. The more common form is "rubbed" sage, crumbled dried leaves, but it is also available ground; rubbed sage has more

(continued on page 260)

SAGE
fresh, ground, rubbed,
and dried whole leaves

SAGE *(continued from page 258)*

flavor and keeps its flavor longer. Bunches of dried Greek sage still on the stems can be found in some specialty markets. Sage is an essential seasoning in the stuffing for the Thanksgiving turkey, of course, and onions sautéed with sage are the base for many savory dishes. It goes well with fatty meats like pork, as well as with game such as duck and goose, and is often used to flavor sausages. Sage is also good in bean dishes and hearty soups and stews. It pairs well with other strong Mediterranean herbs such as rosemary, thyme, oregano, and bay, and it features in many herb blends. Sage Derby, a mild cow's-milk cheese marbled with sage, is a favorite in England.

SALAM LEAVES

BOTANICAL NAME: *Syzygium polyanthum* (formerly *Eugenia polyantha*)
OTHER NAMES: Indonesian bay leaves, daun salam, salaam leaves
FORMS: fresh and dried

Salam leaves are sometimes referred to as Indonesian bay leaves (*daun salam* is their name in Indonesia), but they are in an unrelated species and the flavor is quite different from that of bay laurel leaves. However, the fresh or dried leaves are used in the same ways as true bay leaves. They are common in Indonesian and Malaysian cuisines but are little known outside their native habitat. The dried leaves are aromatic with a mild citrusy, somewhat tart flavor. They are best in soups, stews, and other long-simmered preparations. They also season *nasi goreng,* Indonesia's version of fried rice and its best-known dish.

SALT

Salt is, of course, a mineral, not a spice, but it is a seasoning we can't do without. It's also essential to life; our bodies need salt. And it is one of the four basic tastes: sweet, salty, sour, and bitter (more recently, a fifth taste, umami, has been recognized). The use of salt can be traced back to Neolithic times. It was so highly valued by the early Romans that soldiers were paid in part with salt (the word *salary* comes from the Latin *salarium,* which means, literally, "salt money").

Culinary salts come from the earth or from the sea. Salt from deposits in the earth is also known as rock salt or halite; these deposits were probably formed through the evaporation of ancient seas. Rock salt is usually mined, though a more modern technique is to inject water into the deposits to dissolve the salt, then process and evaporate the resulting saltwater. Sea salt is harvested by various methods, many of them centuries old. The basic process is to evaporate seawater in pools called salt pans or salt ponds, or in salt marshes; see below for more information on the various techniques used to harvest sea salts.

The chemical name for salt is sodium chloride ($NaCl$). All salt is crystalline and dissolves easily when exposed to liquids or moisture. Table salt is simply fine rock salt, usually with additives to keep it from clumping; sometimes iodine is also added, though iodine deficiencies are no longer common in the industrialized world. It can taste harsh or bitter, and good cooks and chefs prefer sea salt. Salt from the sea often contains trace amounts of many other minerals, depending on its place of origin—iodine is one of these, found in all sea salt; see pages 266–272 for more information on the mineral content of various sea salts.

(continued on page 264)

SALT *(continued from page 261)*

Coarse sea salt is usually used as a "finishing salt"—that is, its crystals are sprinkled over a dish, such as grilled meat or fish, just before serving, so they retain their distinctive flavor and crunch. Some sea salts are good as general seasoning salts as well. For those who prefer to grind the salt more finely onto their food, salt grinders are now widely available. Because salt is a mineral, not a spice, grinding it—as opposed to grinding pepper—just before use has nothing to do with the freshness of its flavor; it's all about texture (and appearance).

Salt brings out the flavor of any savory ingredient, but it is also important in cookies, cakes, and other desserts. Sweet baked goods made without salt will taste flat. And the salty-sweet

1. Hickory-Smoked Sea Salt (Fine)
2. Hawaiian Sea Salt (Coarse)
3. Himalayan Pink Salt (Coarse)
4. Himalayan Pink Salt (Fine)
5. Himalayan Pink Salt
6. Sel Gris
7. Alder-Smoked Salt
8. Hickory-Smoked Sea Salt (Coarse)
9. Cyprus Sea Salt
10. Hawaiian Sea Salt (Fine)
11. Trapani Sea Salt
12. Murray River Sea Salt
13. Kosher Salt
14. Maine Sea Salt
15. Applewood-Smoked Sea Salt
16. Peruvian Pink Salt
17. Hawaiian Pink Sea Salt
18. Portugese Sea Salt
19. Cherrywood-Smoked Sea Salt
20. Mesquite-Smoked Sea Salt
21. Fleur De Sel
22. Indian Black Salt
23. Indian Black Salt (Fine)
24. Maldon Smoked Sea Salt
25. Maldon Sea Salt

SALT

264

Smoked sea salt makes a great finishing salt, but it can also be used as an unusual seasoning salt. The salt is cold-smoked over hardwood until intensely fragrant. Alder is one of the most common woods, but apple, hickory, and mesquite are also used; the Maldon company (see page 269) smokes their sea salt over oak. Some French producers offer fleur de sel or other sea salt smoked over the wood from chardonnay wine casks. Applewood-smoked salt is one of the milder choices, but all smoked salts add a distinctive smoky taste to any dish. Sprinkle some over roasted potatoes or a creamy pasta dish, garnish your next Bloody Mary with a pinch of it, or finish pan-seared fish with a smoked salt (in the Pacific Northwest, salmon smoked on planks of alder is classic, making alderwood-smoked sea salt a natural choice for roasted salmon). Or use it in a rub for grilled or roast meat. On the sweeter side, chocolate truffles sprinkled with smoked salt are delicious.

Note that some smoked salts are made with liquid smoke or a similar flavoring and also include additives; be sure to avoid these and choose real smoked salt instead.

contrast appeals to many chocolatiers and consumers—think of the popularity of chocolate-covered caramels garnished with a sprinkling of coarse sea salt, or the now almost ubiquitous salted caramel ice cream.

(continued on next page)

CYPRUS SEA SALT

From the island of Cyprus, this flaky sea salt has unique pyramid-shaped crystals and a mild flavor. It is still harvested using traditional methods. Black Cyprus sea salt, sometimes called black lava salt, gets its color from the addition of activated charcoal (also see Hawaiian Sea Salt, below). Although Cyprus sea salt can be used for general cooking, its unusual shape and its crunch make it an ideal finishing salt.

FLEUR DE SEL

Fleur de sel is a relatively rare sea salt that comes from the coast of Brittany and the offshore islands, also the source of high-quality sel gris (gray salt; see page 271). Its name translates from French as "flower of salt," and it has a lovely floral quality and a pure taste of the ocean. The harvesting process for fleur de sel is even more delicate than that for sel gris. Lighter than gray salt, it floats to the top of the salt flats, and it is removed each day by hand, using small scoops rather than rakes. And, while the harvest for any sea salt is seasonal, the formation of fleur de sel depends on specific climatic conditions, so the harvest is not always reliable. More recently, fleur de sel from Camargue, on France's Mediterranean Coast, has become available, but purists insist that the salt from Brittany is still the best. Crystals of fleur de sel are small, irregular, and moist. It is always used as a finishing salt, sprinkled over dishes both hot and cold.

HAWAIIAN SEA SALT

There are several different types of Hawaiian sea salt, all of which tend to be quite moist. Red Hawaiian sea salt is the most common. Sometimes called alaea salt, it is mixed with a volcanic clay, alaea, that gives it both its color and added minerals, including iron; this traditional technique dates back centuries. Early Hawaiians believed the clay was sacred, and they used red clay salt for religious rituals as well as for medicinal purposes. White Hawaiian sea salt is simply the pure harvested salt. It is sometimes called white silver sea salt or blue sea salt. Black Hawaiian sea salt has a striking black color. Although it is also called volcanic salt or black lava salt, the color actually comes from added activated charcoal. As a result, it is higher in iron than many sea salts. (If you rub it between your fingers, some of the black color will come off.) All these Hawaiian salts can be found in various textures, from large crystals to finely ground. The red and black salts make particularly distinctive finishing salts, especially sprinkled over white-fleshed fish, chicken, or potatoes. They also complement seafood, of course, and can be used as a rub for grilled or roasted whole fish; *poke,* the traditional Hawaiian raw fish dish, is seasoned with alaea sea salt. The red salt is sometimes also used as an everyday table salt in Hawaii.

HIMALAYAN PINK SALT

Himalayan pink salt comes from an enormous ancient mine in the Himalayas, and it is one of the purest salts available. Its color, which ranges from pale to deep pink to rose, comes from iron and other trace minerals (it is stocked in many health food stores because of its high mineral content). The salt is still mined by hand, washed, dried, and ground into crystals of various sizes. Try pink salt when salt-roasting whole fish or chicken, or use it as a finishing salt. It can be ground in a salt grinder (choose a clear one, to show off the color) and used as a seasoning in any type of cooking. Some gourmet markets and other online sources now sell beautiful slabs of Himalayan pink salt that can be used for serving hot or cold food (chill the slab first, in that case), imparting a final touch of seasoning.

(continued on next page)

INDIAN BLACK SALT

Also called Himalayan black salt, and known as *kala namak* in India, this is a rock salt mined primarily in India and Pakistan. It is not, in fact, black but ranges from pinkish-gray or deep violet to amber or dark brown, the color coming from various trace elements, including iron sulfide. It also has a strong sulfurous odor and taste, from the hydrogen sulfide it contains (think rotten eggs), although much of that dissipates in cooking. Black salt is sold as irregular chunks that can be as large as an inch or more across and is also available finely ground; the ground salt may be pink, brown, or gray. The salt is widely used in Indian and Pakistani cooking. It is an essential ingredient in the seasoning blend chaat masala (see page 52), and it adds its distinctive flavor to many savory snacks and street foods. It goes well with seafood, and it can be used to season chutneys or relishes and raita, the yogurt-based condiment. Lemonade spiced with black salt is a popular summer drink in India.

KOSHER SALT

Many chefs and home cooks prefer kosher salt to table salt for everyday use. It is coarse and flaky, making it easy to pick up with your fingers for judicious seasoning, and, unlike ordinary table salt, it doesn't contain additives. It is mild and not as sharp or harsh as table salt; it is also less salty by volume measure (i.e., teaspoon for teaspoon).

MAINE SEA SALT

A number of producers are now harvesting sea salt off the coast of Maine, using traditional methods. The salt is harvested by hand and neither rinsed nor bleached. The irregular crystals are sparkling white and have a clean, briny taste. Maine sea salt is available

CURING SALTS

Curing salts are used for charcuterie and other preserved meats. They are a combination of salt and nitrites, which help prevent the growth of bacteria (such as the potentially deadly *Clostridium botulinum*) in such meats, as well as preserve their rosy color. These salts are always tinted pink to avoid any possible confusion with regular salt, as ingesting more than a tiny quantity of nitrites can be dangerous, and so they are sometimes called pink salt. Other names include Insta Cure #1 and Prague powder. (Hawaiian pink salt and other such pink salts have no relation to curing salts.) Some curing salts, such as Insta Cure #2, also include nitrates; these are usually used for dry-cured sausages, which take longer to cure.

in medium or coarse grinds. It can be ground in a salt grinder for seasoning at the table, or left in whole crystals and used as a finishing salt—great with lobster!

MALDON SEA SALT

Maldon is a large flaky salt that is harvested along England's Atlantic Coast. It has a delicate briny taste and is a favorite among chefs. Maldon is a trademark, and the Maldon Crystal Salt Company is a family business has been producing its salt in Maldon, Essex, since the late nineteenth century. Maldon makes a delicious finishing salt, especially for potatoes and other vegetable dishes and for grilled fish or poultry. The company also produces a smoked version of its salt.

(continued on next page)

MURRAY RIVER SEA SALT

This flaky salt comes from Australia's Murray-Darling Basin in the southeastern state of Victoria. The Murray River is the largest one in Australia and the water in the basin has a high level of salinity; the salt is harvested from underground aquifers. It is a large flaky salt with a lovely pink hue. The flakes are delicate and can even be crushed with your fingertips. The salt dissolves quickly and evenly, and that, in combination with its beautiful color, makes it an excellent finishing salt.

PERUVIAN PINK SALT

Peruvian pink salt comes from underground springs high in the Andes. The salt has been harvested from terraced salt ponds in the Sacred Valley of Incas, near the town of Maras, for centuries, and the same methods are still used today; many of the families here have been salt farmers for generations. (Some packages refer to the salt as *sal de los Incas*.) The coarse crystals are a very pale pink and have a strong mineral flavor and a nice crunch. Sprinkle over salmon or other fish before grilling or pan-roasting it, grind fine for seasoning all sorts of dishes, or use as a finishing salt.

PORTUGUESE SEA SALT

The salt marshes along Portugal's Algarve Coast have long been part of the salt trade, but in recent years, small producers have been working to revive the artisanal production of sea salt there, returning to traditional methods similar to those used in France's Brittany. Portuguese sea salt is white, not gray like Brittany's sel gris, though the hand-harvested salt is not washed or otherwise processed; it can be found as coarse or fine grains and remains very moist. (Traditionally in Portugal, hand-harvested, unprocessed sea salt is called *sal tradicional,* or *sal marinho tradicional,* while machine-harvested salt is called simply *sal do mar*—although it is not unheard of for *sal do mar* to be marketed as *sal tradicional.*) Some artisan producers are also now harvesting *flor de sal,* the Portuguese version of France's fleur de sel, again using age-old methods.

Coarse Portuguese sea salt makes a good rub for grilled meat, fish, or poultry, and both the coarse and fine can be used in general cooking; the coarse salt can also be sprinkled over a finished dish before serving. *Flor de sal,* like fleur de sel, is purely a finishing salt.

SEL GRIS

Sel gris, literally "gray salt," comes from salt marshes or flats along France's Atlantic and Mediterranean Coasts. The best is from Brittany, most notably the town of Guérande, and from the islands of Ré and Noirmoutier. It is still harvested by hand, using long-handled rakes, once the seawater evaporates from the shallow salt pans, and it is not washed or processed at all, so it retains all the minerals found in the seawater. Sel gris is a light gray color and is sold as large irregular crystals or more finely ground. It is a very moist salt, briny and slightly tangy. It is used by many French bakers for their artisan breads, and the finer grinds can be used as a general cooking salt. Potatoes roasted on a bed of coarse sel gris are delicious, moist and delicately seasoned; meats can be rubbed with the salt before roasting. Sel gris can also be used for pickling.

Despite its name, the gray salt known as Celtic sea salt comes from Brittany, which was once one of the six Celtic nations. It is light gray and, like other types of sel gris, moist and briny. It comes in coarse and finer grinds. In 1976, the name Celtic Sea Salt was trademarked by a company called Silena Naturally, which promotes the health benefits of the salt.

French sea salt from the Mediterranean coast, in Camargue

(continued on next page)

and Provence, is usually commercially harvested and washed, and it may contain additives. It is readily available in supermarkets now; look for a brand without additives.

TRAPANI SEA SALT

Trapani sea salt comes from the western coast of Sicily, between Trapani and Marsala. It is still harvested by hand from the salt pans. The salt, which is not washed or otherwise processed, is available as coarse or fine grains. It is slightly off-white, with a briny flavor. In Sicily, it is added to the water for blanching vegetables or cooking pasta; elsewhere, it is more often considered a finishing salt, though the fine salt can be used in general cooking, especially for fish and vegetable dishes.

SAMBAR POWDER

The Tamil word for powder is *podi,* and this South Indian spice blend is usually labeled "sambar powder" (or *sambaar* or *sambhar*) in Indian grocery stores. A classic sambar blend starts with dried chiles and coriander seeds and adds cumin, black pepper, and various dals, or dry-roasted dried lentils—typically chana, toor, or urad dal; a more complicated mix might also include fenugreek, black mustard seeds, and/or turmeric. Some versions add sweeter spices like nutmeg, mace, and cinnamon. There are, of course, simpler versions with far fewer ingredients. Fragrant, spicy sambar powder flavors much of the vegetarian fare of the region, especially soups, dals, and other lentil and vegetable dishes; because of the dried lentils it contains, it also acts as a thickening agent. Sambar is also the name of a lentil and vegetable soup eaten all over South India with rice or dosas and idlis; sambar powder is

(continued on page 274)

SAMBAR POWDER
dried chiles, chana dal, turmeric, cumin, fenugreek, black peppercorns, coriander

always used to season it, and that may be where the name of the blend originated.

SANSHO PEPPER

See Pepper.

SAUNF

See Anise and Fennel.

SAVORY

BOTANICAL NAMES: *Satureja hortensis* (summer savory); *S. montana* (winter savory)
FORMS: fresh and dried leaves

There are two types of savory, a member of the mint family, that are used in cooking: summer, which is an annual, and winter, a perennial. Both are native to the Mediterranean region. Savory is one of the oldest culinary herbs, and the Romans are known to have made a sauce of savory and vinegar. Summer savory, which grows to about 18 inches tall, has small green to dark green leaves and bears white or purple flowers, which are sometimes part of the mix when the herb is dried. It is very fragrant, and its aroma is somewhat peppery, with strong notes of thyme; the taste is also peppery. Winter savory is a smaller plant, with small, shiny, dark green leaves and white flowers when mature; it looks something like thyme at first glance. Its fragrance and flavor are similar to that of summer savory but it has a more pungent bite.

Savory dries well and will keep for months if stored properly. It is sometimes called the bean herb, and it is excellent in dried bean dishes and with other legumes, retaining its flavor even during long simmering. It is also good in stuffings and in sausages and other charcuterie. Generally, the two types can be used interchangeably, but if substituting winter savory in a recipe that calls for the summer herb, you may want to reduce the amount. Savory complements chicken, pork, veal, and beef and can be used in an herb rub or marinade for any of these; it is also good in hearty meat stews. It goes well with trout and other fish, especially when these are grilled. Savory is one of the ingredients in classic herbes de Provence (see page 145).

SESAME

BOTANICAL NAME: *Sesamum indicum*
OTHER NAMES: benne, gingelly, til, teel
FORMS: whole seeds

Sesame is an annual indigenous to northern Africa and, some authorities believe, also native to India. It has been grown in Asia for centuries (although it is still considered a "foreign" plant in China), as well as in Indonesia. It is generally considered to be the oldest crop grown for its oil; the oil content of the seeds is very high. Today, sesame is cultivated primarily in India, China, Indonesia, Africa, Mexico, Guatemala, and the United States. The seeds were brought to the United States by African slaves in the seventeenth and eighteenth centuries, and they are still called *benne,* an African word for "sesame," throughout the American South.

The seedpods, or capsules, that contain sesame seeds tend to

(continued on next page)

shatter easily once ripe, so the seeds must be harvested before they are fully mature. Traditionally, harvesting was done by hand, the stalks cut and then dried and the seeds removed, and it is still done this way in many countries. But more recently, varieties that do not burst when ripe have been developed, allowing for mechanical harvesting. The seeds are small, flat, and oval. White sesame seeds, which are actually a pale cream color, are the most common form. Brown sesame seeds, also called "natural," are unhulled white seeds. The white seeds are sometimes sold toasted, and in that case look like the brown seeds. The white seeds have a faint nutty aroma, while unhulled brown seeds have almost no fragrance; both, however, have a pleasing nutty, slightly sweet flavor. Black sesame seeds, grown in Asia, have little aroma but a richer flavor.

Sesame seeds are used in baked goods in many cuisines and are often sprinkled over flatbreads and other breads, bagels (of course), and breadsticks before baking. They pair well with certain vegetables, particularly asparagus, bok choy, and broccoli, as well as eggplant. In India, the seeds are made into a nutty chutney served with various dishes. Toasting brings out the flavor of the seeds, and they are easily toasted in a dry skillet, just until aromatic; overtoasting can make the seeds, especially the black ones, bitter. In Japan, a mixture of toasted sesame seeds and sea salt, called *gomasio,* is a popular seasoning. Sesame seeds may also be sprinkled over salads or stirred into rice or noodle dishes, and the black seeds make a striking garnish. The ground sesame paste known as tahini, made from hulled white seeds, is ubiquitous in the Middle East, and a similar paste made from toasted seeds is used in Japanese and other Asian cuisines. The seeds are also used in sweet dishes and in confections, notably halvah, the Middle Eastern sweet.

(continued on page 279)

SESAME SEEDS
black, brown, and white seeds

SHICHIMI TOGARASHI

Sesame oil is used in many cuisines, and it keeps well even in hot climates. The oil extracted from white seeds is used as a cooking oil in Western kitchens, while Asian oils, made from toasted seeds, are darker and have a stronger, more nutty flavor; they are more often used in dressings or as a finishing oil or garnish.

MEDICINAL USES: Sesame seeds are high in calcium and in iron, manganese, and zinc. They have a slight laxative effect and are thought to help in digestion. Folk medicine attributes various other benefits—such as stimulating circulation and helping cleanse the liver and kidneys—to the seeds.

SHICHIMI TOGARASHI

Also known as seven-flavor or seven-spice mix, shichimi togarashi is a Japanese seasoning mixture that can be very hot or relatively mild, depending on the proportion of chile included (*togarashi* means "red pepper flakes"). The seven ingredients are red pepper flakes, sansho pepper, black or white sesame seeds, black poppy seeds (or hemp or rape seeds), white poppy seeds, dried orange or tangerine peel, and ground nori (dried seaweed). The texture is fairly coarse, with some of the sesame seeds left whole and tiny bits of dried citrus peel throughout, and the aroma is primarily of chiles, with a faint citrus undertone. In Japan, shichimi togarashi is sprinkled over noodles and added to soups and a variety of other dishes. It is also used as a table condiment, to be sprinkled over tempura, udon or soba noodles, and other preparations as desired.

ST. LUCIE'S CHERRY

See Mahlab.

STAR ANISE

BOTANICAL NAME: *Illicium verum*
OTHER NAMES: Chinese anise, badian
FORMS: whole and ground

Star anise is the seedpod of an evergreen tree native to southern China and North Vietnam; it is a member of the magnolia family. Today, it is grown in India, Japan, and the Philippines, as well as in China and Vietnam. The trees first bear fruit after six years, and they may continue to fruit for as long as one hundred years.

Dried star anise has a striking appearance. It looks like an eight-pointed star, and each canoe-shaped "point" splits open to reveal a hard, shiny tan or brown seed. Several of its various Chinese names translate as "eight points." Like allspice, cloves, and pepper, the spice is harvested before it has ripened and then dried in the sun.

Dried star anise is mahogany to dark reddish-brown in color. It has a pungent warm, sweet, spicy aroma, like that of licorice, and its flavor is similar to that of aniseeds but stronger. Although they are unrelated botanically, aniseeds and star anise both contain the essential oil anethole. Star aniseeds have less flavor than the dried casings that surround them. Ground star anise is made from the whole dried spice. The reddish-brown powder has a warm, pungent aroma and strong licorice flavor, with a hint of cloves and a slight bitterness. Because the dried spice is very hard, if you need ground star anise, it is better to buy it preground rather than attempt to grind it in a mortar and pestle or even a spice grinder. Whole star anise keeps almost indefinitely.

Star anise is an important ingredient in Chinese and Vietnamese cooking, and it also seasons Indian and Indonesian dishes. It is pungent, so it should be used sparingly, whether whole or ground. It pairs well with chicken and other poultry; Chinese cooks often add one or two star anise to the cavity of a chicken before roasting it, and it also flavors red-cooked duck. It is an ingredient in soups and stocks, including Chinese master stocks. Star anise adds fragrance to pho, the classic Vietnamese beef soup, and it also flavors long-cooked stews and braises. In most cuisines, the spice is usually added whole to stews and similar dishes, then removed before serving. In India (*badian* is its Indian name), it is used for biryanis and other rice dishes and in curries. Ground star anise is an ingredient in some curry powders, and it is the dominant flavor of Chinese five-spice powder (see page 79). Unlike most spices, star anise is not well known in the West, although it is used to flavor anisette and some liqueurs.

MEDICINAL USES: The flavor of star anise lingers on the tongue, and it can be chewed as a breath freshener or as an aid to digestion. It is considered a stimulant and diuretic, and it is sometimes used as an antiseptic. In some Eastern cultures, the spice is thought to relieve the ache of rheumatism and to cure colic. Star anise tea is prescribed for sore throats and various other ills.

SUMAC

BOTANICAL NAME: *Rhus coriaria*
FORMS: whole berries and powder

Sumac comes from a shrub native to the Mediterranean, and its history dates to ancient times. The Romans used sumac berries as a souring agent and flavoring before citrus fruits reached the region. Sumac still grows wild around the Mediterranean, including in Sicily and southern Italy; major sources today include Turkey and the Middle East.

Sumac berries, which are about the size of a peppercorn, grow in clusters and turn from green to crimson as they ripen. (There are many varieties of the shrub, and some of them—including many of those used as ornamental bushes in North America—are poisonous, so don't be tempted to harvest sumac berries from your backyard. However, Native Americans traditionally used sumac berries to make a refreshing drink, and they also used both leaves and berries in tobacco mixtures.) The berries are picked by hand when mature but slightly underripe and then dried, still on the stem, in the sun for several days. The fully dried berries range from brick-red to almost purple in color. Although they are sometimes sold whole, they are more often ground to a coarse, slightly moist powder; the best-quality powders are a deep reddish-purple. Sumac has a clean, fruity fragrance and tart, fruity, astringent flavor, with a citrus tang but without the sharpness of lemon juice.

Sumac is widely used in cooking in Turkey and the Middle East, especially in Lebanon, Iran, and Iraq. The dried whole berries must be soaked or ground before use; occasionally, the berries are soaked to soften them and then are strained out, pressed to

(continued on next page)

release all their juices, and the liquid used as part of the cooking medium for a stew or other dish. A simple salad of sliced onions seasoned with ground sumac is popular throughout the Middle East. Sumac flavors kebabs and grilled meats, fish, and chicken, and it is added to marinades for foods that will be roasted or grilled. It can be stirred into yogurt to make a marinade, or the seasoned yogurt can be served on its own as a dip or a condiment. Sumac is also sprinkled over rice, hummus, or baba ghanoush, along with a drizzle of olive oil, as a garnish and flavoring. It is an essential ingredient in the Middle Eastern spice blend za'atar (see page 319).

SZECHUAN PEPPER

See Pepper.

[T]

TABIL

Tabil is a hot, aromatic Tunisian spice mix used to season a wide range of dishes. The word *tabil* means "coriander," and that is one of the main ingredients, along with dried garlic, chile, and caraway; some blends also contain cumin or other spices, and sweet peppers are occasionally included. Tabil is similar to harissa (see page 183), and like harissa, this Tunisian blend is found in other North African countries as well. It can be used as a rub for grilled meats, fish, or poultry, and it adds spice to many soups and stews, as well as couscous. It can also be mixed with olive oil to make a seasoning paste.

TAMARIND

BOTANICAL NAME: *Tamarindus indica*
OTHER NAMES: Indian date, assam, imli, puli
FORMS: blocks, concentrate, and powder

Tamarind is the fruit of a tall tropical evergreen tree in the bean family. It is indigenous to eastern Africa, and possibly also to southern Asia, and it has grown wild in India for centuries. Tamarind was used by the Arabs in the Middle Ages, and the

(continued on page 290)

TAMARIND
block, powder, and dried

TAMARIND *(continued from page 288)*

Europeans also knew it then. Spanish conquistadors took tamarind to Mexico and the West Indies. Today, India is one of the major producers, but tamarind is also cultivated in Thailand and other Asian countries, as well as in Mexico and the East Indies.

Tamarind pods look like fat, dark brown broad beans. They are about 4 inches long, and the pulp contains ten or so hard seeds. The pods are harvested when ripe, often after they have begun to split open. The outer skins are removed, and the sticky reddish-brown pulp, with the seeds intact, is usually shaped into bricks or blocks; the pulp darkens to a very deep brown. Tamarind is also processed into a flavorful (and easier to use) concentrate, made by cooking down the pulp with water and then straining it to remove the seeds and fibers. More recently, tamarind powder has become available.

With a mild fruity fragrance and a tart, sweet, fruity flavor, tamarind is the main souring agent in Indian cooking and is used for the same purpose in other tropical kitchens (one of its names in Asia is *assam,* which means "acid"). To use the pulp, pull off a small chunk from a block of tamarind and soak it in a little hot water for 15 to 20 minutes or so, until it softens, then mash the pulp and liquid together and strain. Tamarind concentrate is ready to be used, and the powder can be stirred into any dish to add a hit of tartness, though the flavor will not be as complex.

In India, tamarind adds its distinctive flavor to a range of curries, dals and other lentil dishes, and chutneys. It is popular in Thailand, where it is used in soups, sauces, and curries. Tamarind is particularly good with fish and seafood. It can be used in desserts and sweets, as well as in savory dishes, and it is made into a refreshing drink in countries from Thailand to East Africa to the Caribbean and Mexico. Tamarind is one of the ingredients in Worcestershire sauce. It can also be used in candies.

MEDICINAL USES: Tamarind is considered a digestive in India, where it is also used to treat various intestinal disorders and to heal wounds. It is high in iron and thiamine, as well as in tartaric acid, an antioxidant.

TARRAGON

BOTANICAL NAMES: *Artemisia dracunculus* (French tarragon);
A. dracunculoides (Russian tarragon)
OTHER NAMES: French tarragon, true tarragon
FORMS: fresh and dried leaves

French tarragon, or true tarragon, is a small perennial indigenous to the Mediterranean; it is a member of the daisy family. Its history is not as long as that of many other herbs, and it was not really known in Europe until around the sixteenth century. Its Latin name means "dragon," as does its Arabic name, *tarkhum;* *estragon,* its French name, means "little dragon." Most sources attribute the origin of the name to a belief that tarragon was an antidote to the venom of poisonous serpents. The other most common variety of the herb is Russian tarragon, which is native to Siberia. It is a taller, straighter plant (French tarragon tends to sprawl), but its leaves have little of the wonderful flavor of true tarragon. Real tarragon has a licorice-like fragrance (it contains the same volatile oil as anise) and a spicy, peppery, green taste. The pots of tarragon sold at the garden market are often Russian tarragon, since French tarragon is more difficult to cultivate and

(continued on page 293)

TARRAGON
fresh and dried

therefore more costly; be sure to check the provenance. Good-quality dried tarragon has the same peppery anise-like flavor, with a slightly sweeter note.

Tarragon is one of the most important herbs in classic French cuisine. It is essential for rémoulade and béarnaise sauce, among others, and it is one of the herbs in the mix known as fines herbes (see page 123). It complements chicken (think chicken tarragon salad) and delicate fish like poached sole; a lemony tarragon butter is a lovely accompaniment to simply prepared fish or seafood. Tarragon is delicious in crab cakes, and it is often one of the herbs in tartar sauce. It's also good in omelets and other egg dishes. Mustard is often flavored with tarragon, and tarragon vinegar has myriad uses. Grapefruit or lemon sorbet infused with tarragon is a refreshing, sophisticated way to end a meal.

TEJ PATTA/TEJPAT

See Cassia Leaves.

THYME

BOTANICAL NAMES: *Thymus vulgaris*; *T. citriodorus* (lemon thyme)
FORMS: fresh and whole or ground dried leaves

Thyme is one of the oldest of all herbs, used in Egypt at the time of the pharaohs and in ancient Greece and Rome. It is a small perennial shrub indigenous to the Mediterranean, most notably the region that extends from southern Europe to North Africa. There are actually dozens of types of thyme, but many of them are purely ornamental. Common thyme, sometimes called garden thyme, is

(*continued on next page*)

the kitchen herb of choice. Lemon thyme also has culinary uses (see below).

Thyme leaves are tiny, pointed, and green; they are very aromatic because they contain thymol, an important essential oil. Their fragrance is warming and spicy, with undertones of pine and citrusy, minty notes (thyme is a member of the mint family); the flavor is also intense and warming, with a faintly medicinal note. The leaves should be stripped from their woody stems before use. Because of the presence of thymol, thyme dries well, retaining much of its pungency (in fact, in arid climates, thyme tends to be at least already partially dried on the stem when it is harvested). The thyme that grows all over Provence and other regions is called *serpolet* in France. The herb known as za'atar (see page 318) in the Middle East is another type of wild thyme.

Thyme is one of the most common herbs in the kitchens of Europe and North America, as well as throughout the Middle East. It is an essential part of any bouquet garni (see page 36), the classic French herb bundle that is used to season stocks, soups, and stews. It is also one of the ingredients in the blend known as herbes de Provence (see page 145). It helps cut the richness of fatty foods such as duck or goose and pork; it is also good with chicken. Thyme complements most vegetables, particularly tomatoes, onions, mushrooms, and root vegetables, and it is an important seasoning in many dried bean dishes.

Lemon thyme deserves to be more well-known than it is. It is less intense than garden thyme, but it has a lovely citrus aroma and flavor. Lemon thyme is particularly suited to desserts such as poached fruit, and it can be used in scones and shortbread. On the savory side, lemon thyme is, not surprisingly, good with fish and shellfish, as well as with chicken.

THYME
fresh, dried, and ground

TUNISIAN FIVE-SPICE MIX
black peppercorns, cloves, cinnamon, nutmeg, and grains of paradise

TUNISIAN FIVE-SPICE MIX

OTHER NAMES: qâlat daqqa, gâlat dagga

Qâlat daqqa is a Tunisian spice mix that combines black pepper, cloves, nutmeg, cinnamon, and grains of paradise, all ground to a fine powder. Its flavor and aroma are warm, sweet, and pungent. It seasons many tagines, meat-based stews, and couscous. It is good with pumpkin and other winter squashes, eggplant, and legumes, particularly chickpeas. Qâlat daqqa can be used as a dry rub for grilled meats or added to marinades for lamb or poultry.

TURMERIC

BOTANICAL NAME: *Curcuma longa*
OTHER NAMES: Madras turmeric, Alleppey turmeric, yellow ginger, Indian saffron
FORMS: ground

A tropical perennial, turmeric is a member of the ginger family and, like ginger, the spice comes from the underground rhizomes of the plant. It is native to India, and today, India is by far the largest producer and exporter, but it is also grown widely in Asia, notably in Indonesia, and in South America and the Caribbean. There are two main types of ground turmeric: Madras and Alleppey. Madras turmeric is primarily grown in the Indian state of Tamil Nadu but gets its name from the fact that it has historically been traded in its capital city of Madras, now called Chennai. Alleppey turmeric comes from Kerala, and its name derives from the Alleppey District near Cochin.

 Turmeric rhizomes are rounder than those of ginger, and

(continued on next page)

they are bright orange inside. To harvest them, whole clumps of the rhizomes are carefully removed from the earth and then the smaller rhizomes, called "fingers" (see Ginger, page 133) are broken off from the larger rhizomes and boiled or steamed. This step helps shorten the drying time and prevents the small rhizomes from sprouting. Then they are dried and polished, removing the skin in the process, before they are ground. The dried rhizomes are rock-hard, so commercial grinding is really a necessity.

Most of the ground turmeric we see is Madras turmeric, and it is bright yellow to orange; Alleppey turmeric, which is darker in color, is considered of higher quality. Both lend color to any dish to which they are added (or to your hands, or cutting board, or clothes—turmeric has been used as a natural dye throughout its long history). The aroma of Madras turmeric is musty and warm, with a slightly bitter undertone; Alleppey is more fragrant and distinctly earthy. Both have a pungent, bitter taste. Marco Polo compared turmeric to saffron, and it is sometimes suggested as a substitute in recipes, but the two spices have nothing in common other than their bright color.

Turmeric is an essential ingredient in Indian curries, and it seasons a vast range of regional dishes throughout the country. It pairs well with vegetables such as cauliflower, celery, and potatoes, as well as with lentils, rice, and noodles, and it complements both

TURMERIC TEA

Bring 4 cups water to a boil in a saucepan, add 1 teaspoon ground turmeric and, if you like, 1½ teaspoons ground ginger, and simmer for 10 minutes. Strain, add 1 cup milk and honey to taste, and stir well.

(continued on page 300)

TURMERIC
dried, fresh, ground Madras,
and ground Alleppey

seafood and poultry. It is added to chutneys, and because it is a preservative, it is used in many pickles. Turmeric is also found in the kitchens of Nepal, South Asia, Morocco, and the Middle East. It is an ingredient in most curry powders and in many tandoori spice blends and often in charmoula (see page 183), as well as in Morocco's ras el hanout (see page 248). Turmeric is widely used as a coloring agent in the food industry, in foods from mustard to cheese.

MEDICINAL USES: Turmeric is important in Ayurvedic medicine and is often infused in boiling water to make a tea (see sidebar, page 298). It is used to relieve gastrointestinal discomfort and to promote digestion. It is also believed to be a remedy for liver disorders and an anti-inflammatory agent for treating chronic illnesses such as asthma, and it is used in ointments and creams as an antiseptic to treat cuts and burns.

URFA CHILE

See Red Pepper Flakes, page 77.

VANILLA

VADOUVAN

VADOUVAN

Vadouvan is an Indian curry powder with a French influence. Its heritage reflects the French colonial presence in the Pondicherry region of southern India, and it derives from a spice blend called *vadavam* or *vadagam*. It differs from traditional curry powders in that it contains onions, garlic, and sometimes shallots. Other ingredients include cumin, coriander, mustard seeds, fenugreek, cardamom, curry leaves, cayenne, and black pepper; some versions contain fennel seeds, and even rosemary, reflecting its French roots. Traditionally, the onions and other aromatics were dried in the sun before they were combined with the rest of the ingredients. In India, vadouvan seasons "French-style" dishes such as braised chicken or curried chicken salad, as well as roasted vegetables and some curries. With its warming curry-spice aroma, mild onion fragrance, and rich savory flavor, it complements legumes and grains, and it adds depth to many soups and stews. It can also be an ingredient in marinades for grilled seafood or poultry. Recently, vadouvan has become trendy among chefs in the United States.

VANILLA

BOTANICAL NAMES: *Vanilla planifolia;* Tahitian vanilla, *V. tahitensis*
FORMS: whole pods, extract, and paste

Vanilla beans are the fruit of a climbing orchid indigenous to Mexico and Central America. They have been harvested in Mexico for centuries, and the Aztecs used vanilla to flavor a chocolate drink. It was only several centuries later that the vines were first grown successfully (see page 306 regarding pollination methods)

(continued on next page)

on the Bourbon Islands, east of southern Africa, most notably Réunion, Madagascar, and Cormoro. Production on Tahiti also began in the 1800s, but Tahitian vanilla is a different species; it is actually a cross between *Vanilla planfolia* and *V. fragrans*. Today, Mexico, Madagascar, Tahiti, and Indonesia are the main producers, but the quality of Indonesian vanilla can vary and it is often considered inferior.

Efforts to grow vanilla in countries other than Mexico were unsuccessful until it was discovered that there the flowers were pollinated by tiny bees of the genus *Melipona* and that the flowers could be pollinated by hand elsewhere. Hand-pollination is only the beginning of the arduous process that results in the seductively fragrant beans we know. The pods are harvested when unripe and still green; when the very tips have begun to turn yellow, they are ready. The pods do not all reach that stage at the same time, so the harvest can extend over a month or more. In Mexico, the green pods are heated in ovens for 24 to 48 hours to begin the curing process; on the Bourbon Islands, they are blanched in boiling water instead. Then the beans are spread out in the sun every morning to dry and at the end of each day are packed into boxes or other containers to sweat overnight. Finally—the entire process can take up to six months—they are stored for a period of time until they are dark brown or black and intensely aromatic. In Tahiti, the pods are picked when mature and dried in a cool place for a week or so, at which point they are rinsed and then subjected to a similar curing process, drying under the sun for much of the day and wrapped and sweated overnight, for up to a month. Then they are stored for two to three months longer to further develop the flavor.

Good vanilla beans are deep brown, plump, flexible, and very aromatic, with a sweet, mellow, floral fragrance. Some pods are covered with white crystals, which is not a bad thing—these are crystallized vanillin, the main flavor component of vanilla. Inside the pod is a sticky pulp composed of hundreds of tiny seeds. For the most flavor, vanilla beans are split before they are added to the liquid they will simmer in and infuse; sometimes the seeds are scraped out and used on their own, or both the pod and seeds may be added (the tiny black specks in high-quality vanilla ice cream are the seeds, which are not strained out; similarly, you may see the tiny seeds at the bottom of a ramekin of crème brûlée). When buying vanilla extract, avoid artificial vanilla at all costs—it has nothing of the flavor of the true extract. Vanilla paste is now also available from specialty producers. It is essentially vanilla seeds in a sweet vanilla syrup and is very fragrant; it can be substituted in the same quantity in any recipe that calls for vanilla extract. All three products should be stored in a cool, dark place; vanilla beans can be stored, well wrapped, in the freezer to keep them fresher and more aromatic.

Vanilla is widely used in cookies and cakes and other desserts, of course—from custard and gelato to poached fruit to chocolates—but it also works in some savory preparations. Lobster in vanilla sauce was one of renowned French chef Alain Senderens's signature dishes in the 1980s, and it has been much copied; other chefs have served sweetbreads or veal in a vanilla sauce.

WASABI

BOTANICAL NAME: *Wasabia japonica*
OTHER NAME: Japanese horseradish
FORMS: powder and paste

Wasabi is often referred to as Japanese horseradish, but the two are actually different plants. Wasabi is a perennial herb in the Brassica family, and it is the rhizome of the plant that is used. In Japan, the plant grows wild in cold mountain streams (its Japanese name means "mountain hollyhock"). It is difficult to cultivate under other conditions, but it is raised commercially in Japan in flooded mountain terraces. More recently in the United States, a handful of producers, primarily on the Pacific Coast, have succeeded in growing fresh wasabi in limited quantities.

Fresh wasabi, however, is still difficult to find in the United States, and it is usually prohibitively expensive. For use, the thick, green fresh rhizomes are trimmed, peeled, and grated. The aroma and flavor are sharp, clean, and sinus clearing. For wasabi powder, the rhizomes are dried and finely ground. The powder is often mixed with ground dried horseradish and sometimes mustard, but it is possible to find pure ground wasabi—for a price. Recently, fresh wasabi paste has become available from a handful of producers. Otherwise, instead of the prepared wasabi paste that is typically sold in small tubes, it is better to make your own paste with powdered wasabi and water, as the commercial paste usually includes artificial coloring and other additives. After mixing up a batch, be sure to let the paste stand for at least 10 minutes to bring out the flavor.

Wasabi paste is a traditional accompaniment to sashimi, often mixed with a soy dipping sauce, and it is used in many forms

(continued on next page)

of sushi. It is also served with various fish dishes. The powder can be combined with other ingredients to make a spicy seasoning rub or marinade. And wasabi paste can be stirred into mayonnaise for a pungent sauce.

MEDICINAL USES: Wasabi is believed to have anti-inflammatory and antibiotic properties.

WILD CELERY

See Radhuni.

WILD LIME

See Kaffir Lime Leaves.

[Y]

YERBA SANTA

See Hoja Santa.

ZA'ATAR

BOTANICAL NAME: *Thymbra spicata*
OTHER NAMES: wild mountain thyme, Lebanese oregano, Syrian marjoram
OTHER SPELLINGS: Zahtar
FORMS: fresh and dried leaves

The herb za'atar, not to be confused with the Middle Eastern spice mix of the same name (see next page), is a type of wild thyme that grows on hillsides and mountains in the eastern and southern Mediterranean regions. It has a pungent aroma and an intense flavor that is something like that of a mix of oregano, thyme, and marjoram—hence some of its other common names. Za'atar, which retains its herbal pungency when dried, is included in most but not all versions of the spice blend. Mixed with other herbs or seasonings, it makes a good rub for grilled meats, such as lamb, and poultry; it can also be added to marinades for grilled fish, meat, or poultry. Dried za'atar is very good blended with olive oil and drizzled over flatbreads. The fresh herb is often an ingredient in the fillings for *borek,* the savory phyllo-dough pastry popular in Turkey and many Middle Eastern countries.

ZA'ATAR

OTHER SPELLINGS: Zahtar

Za'atar is an aromatic spice mix that is popular throughout the Middle East. (Somewhat confusingly, *za'atar* is also the word for wild thyme; see above.) The blend has many variations, depending on the cook and the region. The most basic version is made with thyme, sumac, toasted sesame seeds, and usually salt, but other spices such as coriander or herbs such as marjoram may be included. Za'atar is delicious sprinkled over warm flatbreads that have been brushed with olive oil; it is often incorporated into flatbread doughs before baking. In Syria, some families bring their own custom blends to their neighborhood bakery for their breads. Za'atar can be mixed with oil and brushed over baked breads or served as a dip or condiment. It is also used as a seasoning for kebabs, and it can be sprinkled over or stirred into labneh or strained yogurt.

ZEDOARY

BOTANICAL NAMES: *Curcuma zedoaria, C. zerumbet*
OTHER NAMES: wild turmeric, amb halad
FORMS: dried slices and ground

Zedoary is a rhizome that is related to ginger, galangal, and turmeric. Sources differ as to its origins—India, Indonesia, China, and/or Southeast Asia—but today it primarily grows in India and Indonesia, and it is little known beyond these regions. There are two types of zedoary, distinguished only by their shape: *C. zedoaria* rhizomes are round and fat, looking more like ginger, and

(continued on next page)

C. zerumbet is longer and thinner, resembling turmeric. *Amb halad* is its common Indian name, though it is also known as *manga inji*, meaning "mango ginger." It is sometimes called *kentjur* or *kencur* in Indonesia, but that name is more correctly applied to a type of galangal.

Zedoary is harvested in much the same way as turmeric (see page 297), but it is usually sliced before drying, to speed up the process. The skin of the fresh rhizome is tan or yellowish and the interior is yellow. Dried sliced zedoary is grayish-brown; ground zedoary is light brown. The aroma is warm, musky, and similar to that of ginger, with an undertone of camphor; the taste is very similar to that of ginger. (Fresh zedoary sometimes has the fragrance of mangoes—*amb* is the word for mango in many parts of India.)

Zedoary is an old spice, and it was used in European kitchens in the Middle Ages, but it is more difficult to cultivate than ginger or galangal, and both of these came to be favored over zedoary. It is still used in seafood curries and some other dishes in Southeast Asia, especially Indonesia, and in southern India. Ground zedoary, called *shoti* in parts of India, is used as a thickener in various dishes. Zedoary extract is an ingredient in Swedish bitters, a traditional herbal tonic.

MEDICINAL USES: Zedoary is a digestive and is also used to relieve indigestion, nausea, and other types of gastrointestinal distress. An "instant tea" made with ground zedoary and boiling water is often recommended for such complaints.

ZERESHK

See Barberry.

ZHUG/ZHOUG

See Charmoula and Other Spice Pastes, page 183.

ACKNOWLEDGMENTS

This book could not have been published without my dear friend and editor Daniel Halpern and my agent, Luke Janklow. A heap of gratitude goes to the great Judith Sutton for her tireless research and dedicated thoroughness. Additional thanks go to the good folks at Ecco, including Bridget Read, Ashley Garland, Suet Chong, and Rachel Meyers, as well as Evan Sung for his stunning photography. My thanks also to Nidhi Bhatt and Anthony Jackson for helping me juggle all the balls in the air. Thank you to Francine Prose, Susan Roxborough, and Racha Haroun, each of whom generously looked over things when I needed a second or even third opinion. And, of course, a special thanks to Aziz Osmani who, wanting a book to represent Kalyustan's, his beloved and iconic store, encouraged me for years and waited patiently until I could find the right way to do it. Thank you also to all the various Kalyustan's staff members, including Dona Abramson, and owners, including Sayedul Alam, over the years for helping me to enrich my palate and fill my family's plates full of flavors from around the world.

And last, a huge thank-you to my foremothers: my grandmother Rajima; my mother, Vijaya; and my aunts, Banu and Neela, for passing down to me their knowledge of ingredients and their collective decades of wisdom and experience at the stove.

Thank you for nurturing, little by little, a lifelong passion for spices, for cultivating an unending curiosity in the kitchen. You have given me the greatest gift. I could not have written this book for Krishna without all of you.

Alford, Jeffrey, and Naomi Duguid, *Hot Sour Salty Sweet: A Culinary Journey Through Southeast Asia* (New York: Artisan, 2000).

——, *Mangoes and Curry Leaves: Culinary Travels Through the Great Subcontinent* (New York: Artisan, 2005).

Andrews, Jean, *Red Hot Peppers* (New York: Macmillan, 1993).

Bharadwaj, Monish, *The Indian Spice Kitchen: Essential Ingredients and Over 200 Authentic Recipes* (New York: Dutton, 1997).

Bayless, Rick, with Deann Groen Bayless, *Authentic Mexican: Regional Cooking from the Heart of Mexico* (New York: Morrow, 1987).

Daley, Simon, with Roshan Hirani, *Cooking with My Indian Mother-in-Law* (London: Pavilion, 2008).

Floyd, David, *The Hot Book of Chilies* (London: New Holland, 2006).

Hemphill, Ian, *The Spice and Herb Bible: A Cook's Guide* (Toronto: Robert Rose, 2000).

Herbst, Sharon Tyler, and Ron Herbst, *The New Food Lover's Companion*, 4th ed. (Hauppauge, NY: Barron's, 2007).

Hill, Tony, *The Contemporary Encyclopedia of Herbs and Spices: Seasonings for the Global Kitchen* (Hoboken, NJ: Wiley, 2004).

Jinich, Pati, *Pati's Mexican Table: The Secrets of Real Mexican Home Cooking* (New York: Houghton Mifflin Harcourt, 2013).

Jordan, Michele Anna, *The Good Cook's Book of Mustard, with More Than 100 Recipes* (Boston: Addison-Wesley, 1994).

——, *Salt and Pepper: 135 Perfectly Seasoned Recipes* (New York: Broadway, 1999).

Kennedy, Diana, *From My Mexican Kitchen: Techniques and Ingredients* (New York: Potter, 2003).

Lahlou, Mourad, *Mourad: New Moroccan* (New York: Artisan, 2011).

Leite, David, *The New Portuguese Table: Exciting Flavors from Europe's Western Coast* (New York: Potter, 2009).

Malouf, Greg, and Lucy Malouf, *Artichoke to Za'atar: Modern Middle Eastern Food* (Oakland, CA: University of California Press, 2006).

McGee, Harold, *On Food and Cooking: The Science and Lore of the Kitchen*, rev. ed. (New York: Scribner, 2004).

Miller, Mark, with John Harrisson, *The Great Chile Book* (Berkeley, CA: Ten Speed, 1991).

Mowe, Rosalind, ed., *Southeast Asian Specialties: A Culinary Journey* (New York: Könemann, 1998).

Norman, Jill, *The Complete Book of Spices: A Practical Guide to Spices and Aromatic Seeds* (New York: Dorling Kindersley, 1990).

Ortiz, Elisabeth Lambert, *The Complete Book of Caribbean Cooking* (New York: Ballantine, 1973).

——, *The Encyclopedia of Herbs, Spices, and Flavorings: A Cook's Compendium* (New York: Dorling Kindersley, 1992).

Prudhomme, Paul, *Chef Paul Prudhomme's Louisiana Kitchen* (New York: Morrow, 1984).

Roden, Claudia, *The Book of Jewish Food: An Odyssey from Samarkand to New York* (New York: Knopf, 1996).

——, *The New Book of Middle Eastern Food* (New York: Knopf, 2000).

Santibañez, Roberto, *Rosa's New Mexican Table* (New York: Artisan, 2007).

Sortun, Ana, *Spice: Flavors of the Eastern Mediterranean* (New York: Regan, 2000).

Stobart, Tom, *Herbs, Spices, and Flavorings* (New York: Overlook, 1982).

Traunfeld, Jerry, *The Herbfarm Cookbook* (New York: Scribner, 2000).

Tsuji, Shizuo, *Japanese Cooking: A Simple Art*, rev. ed. (New York: Kodansha, 2006).

Villas, James, *The Glory of Southern Cooking* (Hoboken, NJ: Wiley, 2007).

Von Welanetz, Diana and Paul, *The Von Welanetz Guide to Ethnic Ingredients: How to Buy and Prepare More Than 1,000 Foods from Around the World* (New York: Warner, 1982).

Wolfert, Paula, *The Food of Morocco* (New York: Ecco, 2011).

Yu, Su-Mei, *Cracking the Coconut: Classic Thai Home Cooking* (New York: Morrow, 2000).

WEBSITES

www.gummastic.gr (Chios Mastiha Growers Association)

www.nielsenmassey.com

www.patismexicantable.com

www.seriouseats.com

INDEX

Italicized page numbers indicate photos

A

achiote. *See* annatto
advieh (adwiya), 2, 4–5
African bird's eye chiles. *See* piri
    piri chiles
ají amarillo (ají mirasol) chiles,
    56–57, *60*
ají panca chiles, 58, *60*
ajmud (ajmod). *See* radhuni
ajowan, *3*, 5–6
    Tea, 6
Aleppo chiles, *76*, 77. *See also* red
    pepper flakes
allspice, 2, 8–9
    Tea, 8
amchur, 2, *10*, 11
anardana, 2, 12, *13*
ancho chiles, 58–59, *61*
anise (aniseed), *3*, 15–17
    Tea, 16
annatto (achiote), *3*, 17–18
    Oil, 18
Armenian spice mix (chaimen),
    3, 18–19
asafoetida, *3*, 19–20

B

baharat, *23*, 24, *25*
barberry, *22*, 26–27
basil, *22*, 27–29, *28*
    subja (sweet basil seeds), 29
bay leaves, *22*, 30–31
Bengali five-spice mix. *See* panch
    phoron
benne seeds. *See* sesame
berbere, *22*, 31–32
bird's beak (de árbol) chiles, 64,
    66
bird's-eye chiles, 59, *61*, 74
black cumin, 93–94
black lemon. *See* black lime
black lime, *23*, 32–34, *33*
black onion seeds. *See* nigella
blends, spice, 95–98
    advieh (adwiya), 2, 4–5
    Armenian, *3*, 18–19
    baharat, *23*, 24, *25*
    berbere, *22*, 31–32
    chaat masala, *41*, 52, *53*, 268
    Chinese five-spice powder, *40*,
        79, 232

Hungarian paprika, *213*, 217,
   218, 219
hyssop, *142*, 146

I

Indian black (Himalayan black)
   salt, *262*, 268
Indonesian bay leaves. *See* salam
   leaves
Indonesian lime. *See* kaffir lime
   leaves

J

Jamaica pepper. *See* allspice
Jamaican jerk seasoning, *182*,
   184
Japanese horseradish. *See* wasabi
japonés chiles, *67*, 68
jeera. *see* caraway; cumin
jerk seasoning, Jamaican, *182*,
   184
juniper, *150*, 151–53

K

kaffir lime leaves, *156–57*,
   158–60, *159*
kalongi. *See* nigella
kapok buds. *See* marathi moggu
Kashmiri chiles, *66*, 68
Kashmiri masala, *156*, 160
kencur (kenchur), 130–31
kewra, 217
khmeli-suneli, *156*, 161

Kirmizi chiles, *76*, 78. *See also* red
   pepper flakes
kokum, *157*, 161–63, *162*
kosher salt, *263*, 268

L

la kama, *166*, 168
Lampong pepper, 226
lavender, *166*, 168–70, *169*
lemon thyme, 294
lemon verbena, *166*, 170–71
lemongrass, *167*, *172*, 173
licorice root, *166*, 173–75
long pepper, 225, 231
loomi. *See* black lime

M

mace, *179*, 180, *181*, 185. *See also*
   nutmeg
Madras curry powder, *96*, 98, *99*
mahlab, *178*, 185–86
Maine sea salt, *262*, 268–69
makrut. *See* kaffir lime leaves
Malabar (Alleppey) pepper, 226
malagueta chiles, 69, *73*. *See also*
   piri piri chiles
Malaysian curry powder, *96*,
   97–98
Maldon sea salt, *263*, 269
mango, dried green. *See* amchur
Maras (Marash) chiles, 77–78,
   78. *See also* red pepper flakes
marathi moggu, *178*, 187
marjoram, *179*, 187–88

PADMA LAKSHMI is the Emmy-nominated host and executive producer of the Bravo series *Top Chef,* and the author of two cookbooks, *Tangy, Tart, Hot & Sweet* and the award-winning *Easy Exotic,* along with the *New York Times* bestselling food memoir *Love, Loss, and What We Ate.* Lakshmi has contributed to such magazines as *Vogue, Gourmet,* and *Harper's Bazaar* (UK and US), and penned a syndicated column on fashion and food for the *New York Times.* Her television-hosting credits include *Planet Food* and *Padma's Passport,* as well as other programs in the United States and abroad. She lives in New York City with her daughter.

JUDITH SUTTON is the author of several cookbooks, including *Sweet Gratitude* and *Champagne & Caviar & Other Delicacies.* She has edited and consulted on dozens of cookbooks for most of the major New York City publishers.